A DLT-Based Trusted Data Exchange Framework for the Ecosystem of Healthcare Things

ASHER

A DLT-Based Trusted Data Exchange Framework for the Ecosystem of Healthcare Things

First Edition April 2025

Written by Asher

TABLE OF CONTENTS

CHAPTER 1

INTRODUCTION

1.1 Internet of Things

The IoT has emerged as a transformative technology, revolutionizing various sectors by connecting physical objects to the internet, enabling them to collect and exchange data. This interconnected network of devices, sensors, and other gadgets has the potential to reshape industries, enhance efficiency, and improve our daily lives. At its core, the IoT operates on the principle of connectivity, allowing devices to communicate and interact seamlessly. These devices can range from simple household appliances like thermostats and refrigerators to complex industrial machinery and infrastructure systems. By embedding sensors and actuators into these objects, IoT enables them to gather real-time data, process information, and even make autonomous decisions.

One of the best things about IoT is that it can make places smarter. IoT systems can improve resource use, predict maintenance needs, and make processes more efficient by collecting and analyzing data. For example, in smart healthcare, IoT devices such as wearable sensors and medical implants can continuously monitor patients' vital signs, allowing healthcare providers to remotely track their health status in real-time. This enables early detection of potential health issues and facilitates timely interventions, reducing the need for frequent hospital visits and improving patient outcomes (Ji et al. 2019).

However, along with its myriad opportunities, the IoT also presents challenges, particularly regarding security and privacy. With a growing number of connected devices, the possibility of cyber threats and data breaches escalates. Businesses and consumers alike need to make sure that sensitive information is kept safe and that IoT systems work properly. The IoT immense promise for transforming industries and enhancing efficiency. By leveraging the power of connectivity and data analytics, the IoT has the potential to revolutionize how we live, work, and interact with the world around us. Nevertheless, addressing security concerns and establishing robust governance frameworks are essential for unlocking the full potential of this groundbreaking technology.

1.1.1 IoT Architecture

The architecture of the IoT encompasses various components that work together to enable the seamless integration of devices, sensors, and applications. Fig.1.1 is a comprehensive overview of the architecture of IoT. IoT is built up of many networks that work together. They are the network layer and the sensors' connection. Sensing systems, such as sensors, actuators, RFID tags, and more, are in this layer. It also handles sensing and recognition. Then it needs help with the gateway and network layers. There are gateway methods that are wrapped up in this layer. As part of its management service layer, the device is modeled, set up, and managed, and security and dataflow are controlled. After that, the application layer is where any real-world business applications in different areas live. In the subsequent section, there is more information about how different types of businesses use IoT (Ahad et al. 2019).

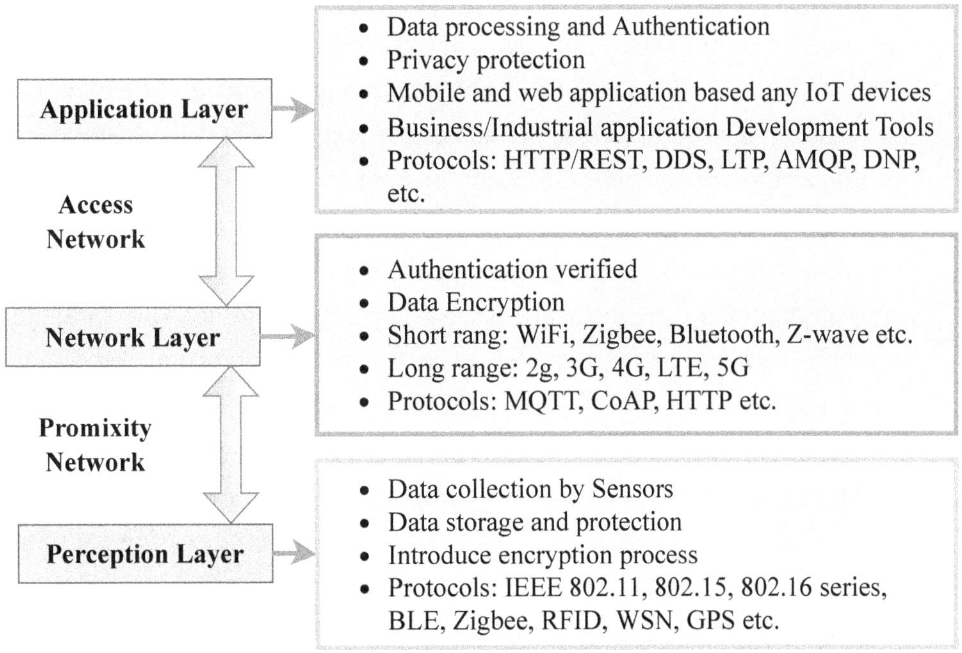

Fig. 1.1 Architecture of IoT (Tahsien et al. 2020).

Application Layer: In IoT architecture, the application layer plays a crucial role in health monitoring systems by facilitating the collection, processing, and interpretation of data from various sensors and devices deployed in healthcare environments. At this layer, software applications are designed to analyze real-time health data, such as vital signs, patient activity, and medication adherence, to provide actionable insights and support clinical decision-making. These applications may employ machine learning algorithms for anomaly detection, predictive analytics, and personalized health recommendations. Additionally, interoperability standards such as enable seamless integration with electronic health records and other healthcare information systems, ensuring efficient data exchange and continuity of care. Overall, the application layer in health monitoring IoT architecture plays a pivotal role in enabling proactive healthcare interventions, improving patient outcomes, and enhancing the efficiency of healthcare delivery.

Network Layer: In health monitoring IoT architecture, the network layer plays a fundamental role in ensuring seamless communication and data exchange between various components of the system. At this layer, IoT devices, sensors, and gateways are interconnected through wired or wireless networks, facilitating the transmission of health data to centralized servers or cloud platforms for further processing and analysis. Network protocols such as MQTT, CoAP, and HTTP are commonly utilized to establish communication links and enable efficient data transfer while considering factors like bandwidth, latency, and reliability. Additionally, security mechanisms such as encryption, authentication, and access control are implemented to safeguard sensitive health information during transit, mitigating the risk of unauthorized access or data breaches. Overall, the network layer in the health monitoring IoT architecture plays a critical role in establishing robust connectivity and ensuring the secure and reliable transmission of health data for timely clinical decision-making and patient care management.

Perception Layer: In health monitoring IoT architecture, the perception layer serves as the foundation for capturing and acquiring health-related data from various sensors, wearable, and medical devices. This layer is responsible for collecting real-time physiological parameters such as heart rate, blood pressure, temperature, and activity levels, among others, from patients or individuals under monitoring. Sensors embedded in wearable devices or integrated into medical equipment capture these data points, which are then transmitted to the network layer for further processing and analysis. Additionally, the perception layer may include preprocessing algorithms to filter and aggregate raw sensor data before transmission, ensuring data accuracy and efficiency. Overall, the perception layer forms the initial stage of the health monitoring process, providing essential input for subsequent layers to derive insights, make informed decisions, and deliver personalized healthcare interventions.

By integrating these layers cohesively, IoT architectures enable the seamless connectivity, data exchange, and interoperability required to support a wide range of applications and use cases. However, designing and implementing robust IoT architectures require careful consideration of factors such as scalability, interoperability, security, and regulatory compliance to ensure the success and sustainability of IoT deployments.

1.1.2 Applications of IoT

The IoT could have a big effect on how people live, the environment, and the economy. Some ideas that are based on the Internet of Things are autonomous vehicles, the smart grid, smart homes and buildings, monitoring public safety and the environment, medical and healthcare, industrial processing, farming and breeding, and living on your own. There is some way that all of these apps are connected to us. The usefulness of these apps and their clear advantages play a big part, and now people are very dependent on them. In recent years, their existence and usefulness have reached a visionary level and are now the most important things in the world (Han et al. 2021). IoT is a concept and vision that drives us into the future, so it might not be wrong to say that it is the only thing that will shape the future of the Internet. Fig.1.2 shows a number of different ways that IoT can be used. The section discusses the IoT based on the functional aspects of applications.

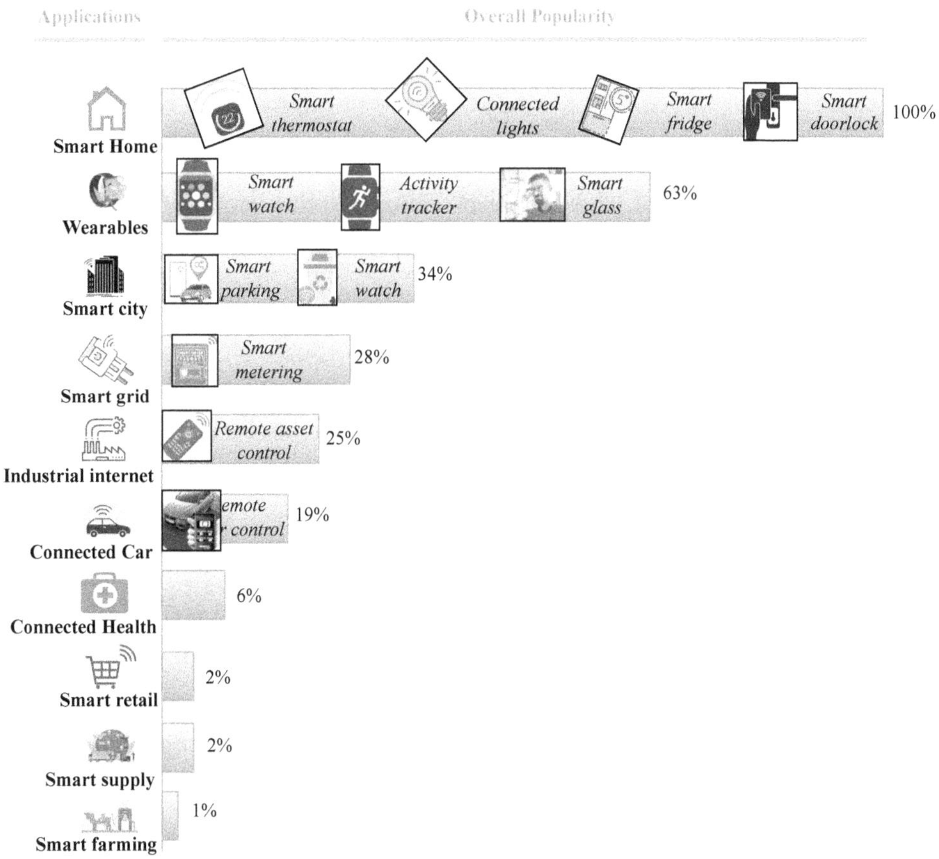

Fig. 1.2 Application of IoT

Smart Home Automation: IoT enables the interconnection of various devices within homes, allowing for centralized control of appliances, lighting, security systems, and heating/cooling systems. Users can remotely monitor and manage their homes via smartphone apps or voice commands, enhancing convenience, energy efficiency, and security.

Industrial Internet of Things (IIoT): In industrial settings, IoT facilitates the integration of sensors, machines, and systems to optimize operations, monitor equipment health, and improve productivity. IIoT applications include predictive maintenance, real-time asset tracking, supply chain optimization, and remote monitoring of production processes.

Smart Cities: IoT technologies are instrumental in building smart cities by enhancing urban infrastructure, transportation systems, and public services. IoT sensors installed in streetlights, traffic signals, waste management systems, and public transportation enable data collection for traffic management, waste optimization, environmental monitoring, and efficient resource allocation.

Healthcare Monitoring: IoT devices such as wearable fitness trackers, medical sensors, and remote patient monitoring systems enable continuous health monitoring outside of traditional clinical settings. These devices can track vital signs, medication adherence, and disease symptoms, providing valuable insights for personalized healthcare management and early intervention.

Agricultural IoT (AgriTech): IoT solutions in agriculture improve crop yields, optimize resource usage, and enable precision farming practices. IoT sensors deployed in fields collect data on soil moisture, temperature, humidity, and crop health, enabling farmers to make data-driven decisions regarding irrigation, fertilization, and pest control.

Retail and Supply Chain Management: IoT technologies streamline inventory management, supply chain logistics, and retail operations. RFID tags, beacons, and sensors track inventory levels, monitor product movement in real-time, and optimize warehouse operations, reducing stockouts, minimizing shrinkage, and enhancing overall operational efficiency.

Energy Management: IoT enables the monitoring and control of energy consumption in residential, commercial, and industrial settings. Smart meters, energy analytics platforms, and IoT-enabled appliances help users track and optimize energy usage, reduce costs, and minimize environmental impact by promoting energy-efficient behaviors and renewable energy integration.

Environmental Monitoring: IoT sensors and devices are deployed for environmental monitoring applications, including air quality monitoring, water quality management, and climate change mitigation. These IoT solutions collect real-time data on pollution levels, weather patterns, and ecological parameters, enabling governments and organizations to implement proactive measures for environmental conservation and sustainability.

Fleet Management and Logistics: IoT-enabled telematics systems and GPS tracking devices are widely used in fleet management and logistics operations. These solutions provide real-time visibility into vehicle location, performance, and driver behavior, optimizing route planning, scheduling, and vehicle maintenance to improve efficiency, reduce fuel consumption, and enhance safety.

Smart Building Management: IoT technology is leveraged to optimize building operations and enhance occupant comfort and safety. Building automation systems integrate IoT sensors and actuators to control lighting, HVAC systems, security systems, and access controls, optimizing energy usage, improving indoor air quality, and ensuring compliance with safety regulations.

These applications demonstrate the diverse ways in which IoT is being utilized to improve efficiency, enhance safety, and enable innovation across various sectors without copying content.

1.1.3 Characteristics of IoT Networks

Heterogeneity: Within an IoT network, an extensive range of devices that possess distinct functionalities, attributes, and communication protocols engage in communication with one another. To be more precise, the devices may employ distinct communication protocols, standards, and paradigms (e.g., cellular or Ethernet), while also being subject to varying limitations on hardware resources. While this heterogeneity facilitates cross-platform communication between various devices, it also presents the IoT network with novel challenges.

Massive deployment: There is a prediction that the capabilities of the current Internet will be surpassed by the billions of devices interconnected and accessible via the Internet. Furthermore, the implementation of IoT on a vast scale presents obstacles. The design of networking and storage architecture for intelligent devices, the implementation of efficient data communication protocols, the proactive detection and defense of IoT against malevolent attacks, the standardization of technologies, and the development of application and device interfaces are a few of these obstacles.

Inter-connectivity: It is anticipated that IoT devices will be interconnected with the worldwide information and communication infrastructure, enabling them to be accessed remotely and at any moment. The type of application and service that the IoT service provider offers determines the connectivity. Connectivity may be local in certain circumstances (as in the case of connected vehicle technology or a swarm of sensors), but global in others (as in the case of smart home access via mobile infrastructure and critical infrastructure management, for instance).

Communication in close proximity: Another notable aspect of IoT is its ability to facilitate communication in close proximity without relying on central authorities like base stations. Device-to-Device (D2D) communication utilizes technologies such as Dedicated Short Range Communication (DSRC) to leverage the benefits of point-to-point communication. Unlike the traditional Internet architecture, which primarily favors network-centric communication, the separation of networks and services allows for both device-centric and content-centric communication in IoT. This diversification enriches the spectrum of IoT services available.

Ultra-Reliable and Low Latency Communication (URLLC): This characteristic of IoT networks becomes crucial in critical real-time applications like industrial process automation, remote surgery, and intelligent transportation systems. In such scenarios, the primary performance limitations revolve around both delay and reliability factors.

Low-power and low-cost communication: Massive connectivity of IoT devices requires ultra low-power and low cost solutions for efficient network operations.

Self-organization and self-healing characteristics: These capabilities are essential for urgent and modern IoT communication, particularly in emergency or disaster scenarios. In such critical situations, depending on the network infrastructure is not feasible, thus necessitating the deployment of self-organizing networks.

Dynamic changes in the network: The IoT encompasses a vast array of devices that require efficient management. These devices operate dynamically; for example, their sleep and wakeup schedules may vary depending on the application. They determine when to utilize the Internet and when to engage in direct communication, adapting to the needs of the situation.

Safety: Safety concerns extend to both consumers and devices due to the sheer volume of IoT devices connected to the Internet. This interconnectedness raises the risk of compromising personal data shared through these devices. Furthermore, privacy and the security of device itself is also an important factor. Intelligence: One of the most fascinating attributes of the IoT is its intelligence, which enables timely and informed decisions to be made based on processed data.

1.2 Internet of Medical Things

In recent years, the healthcare industry has witnessed a significant transformation, largely propelled by advancements in technology. One such transformative force is the IoMT, a network of interconnected medical devices and applications aimed at revolutionizing patient care, clinical workflows, and healthcare delivery. IoMT represents the convergence of medical devices, software applications, and healthcare systems, all interconnected through the internet to collect, transmit, and analyze health data in real-time as showing Fig.1.3.

At its core, IoMT leverages the power of connectivity to enable seamless communication between medical devices, healthcare providers, and patients. By integrating sensors, actuators, and communication technologies into medical devices, IoMT empowers

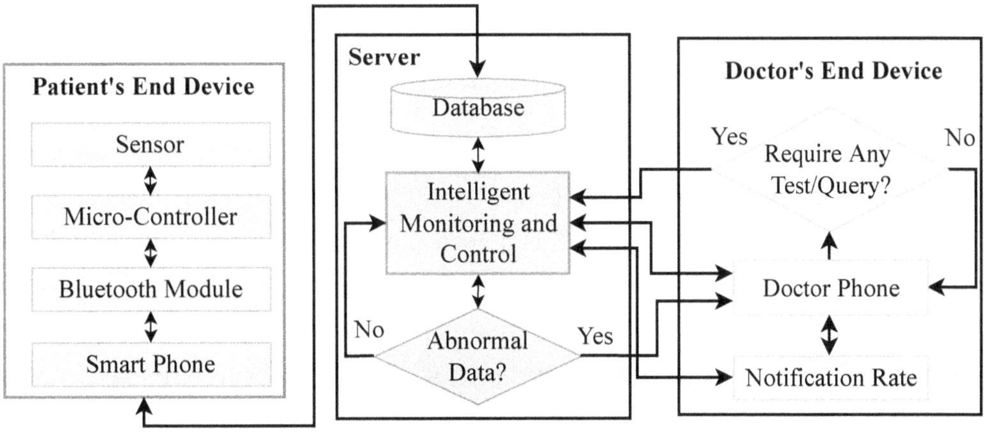

Fig. 1.3 Remote health monitoring system - Architecture.

healthcare professionals with actionable insights, facilitates remote patient monitoring, and enhances the efficiency of healthcare delivery (Karie et al. 2021).

The healthcare industry has always been at the forefront of technological innovation, striving to provide the best possible care to patients. However, in an era marked by the explosive growth of data and the increasing complexity of healthcare systems, new challenges and opportunities have emerged. The convergence of the IoT and blockchain technologies has emerged as a pivotal moment in healthcare, offering unprecedented potential to address these challenges.

1.2.1 Healthcare in the Digital Age

The digitalization of healthcare has led to the creation of vast repositories of patient data, from electronic health records to real-time physiological data gathered through wearable devices. While this digital transformation has the potential to revolutionize patient care, it has also brought to the forefront critical issues surrounding data security, privacy, and interoperability. Healthcare data is incredibly sensitive, encompassing not only medical histories but also personal and demographic information. Ensuring the confidentiality, integrity, and availability of this data is paramount to maintain patient trust and comply with regulations such as the Health Insurance Portability and Accountability Act (HIPAA) and the General Data Protection Regulation (GDPR).

Healthcare is a domain that profoundly impacts individuals from all walks of life. Over time, it has witnessed the integration of numerous techniques and technologies, including information and communication technology (ICT), aimed at enhancing healthcare services. Among these advancements, the Internet of Things stands out as a transformative technology, amalgamating various technologies to bridge the physical and digital realms. The advent of wearable devices and innovations such as Radio Frequency Identification (RFID), Near Field Communication (NFC), Wireless Sensor Networks (WSN), Wireless Sensor and Actuator Networks (WSAN), cloud computing, mobile cloud computing, web services, service-oriented architecture (SOA), smart homes, Web 2.0, Web 3.0, and gateway technologies has facilitated seamless integration across diverse domains, fostering innovative solutions. Through the synergistic application of these technologies, the IoT holds immense potential to revolutionize healthcare delivery. Achieving realistic integration of IoT with healthcare units can lead to unparalleled quality in healthcare services. Leveraging IoT as a diversified technology amalgamation enables remote health monitoring and opens new avenues for improving healthcare outcomes..

Digital technology has significantly transformed our daily routines and communication methods. Upholding paper-based patient records within healthcare establishments can be arduous over time. Electronic health records are utilized in healthcare systems to facilitate the seamless exchange of information. Electronic health record systems have the potential to fully digitize the healthcare system by utilizing clinical information to assist healthcare providers in delivering superior patient care.

One of the primary advantages of IoMT is its ability to revolutionize patient care through remote monitoring and personalized medicine. With wearable devices, implantable sensors, and remote monitoring systems, healthcare providers can continuously collect vital health data, such as heart rate, blood pressure, glucose levels, and activity levels, from patients in real-time. This constant stream of data enables early detection of health issues, personalized treatment plans, and proactive interventions, ultimately improving patient outcomes and reducing healthcare costs. The overview of the internet of medical things model for smart health control systems is presented in Fig.1.4.

The process begins with collecting the patient's vital signs and patient details using different sensors and wearable devices. The collected data is stored on a cloud server. In the event of an emergency situation involving the patients. The cloud sends it to the data base station. The data is verified, and the access control is the medical server. Medical sever sent an alert to the hospital. Hospital staff are taking care of the patient's health situation.

Furthermore, IoMT facilitates the seamless exchange of information across various healthcare stakeholders, including patients, caregivers, healthcare providers, and payers. Through interconnected electronic health records, telemedicine platforms, and health information exchanges, IoMT streamlines communication and collaboration, ensuring timely access to critical patient data and fostering interdisciplinary care coordination.

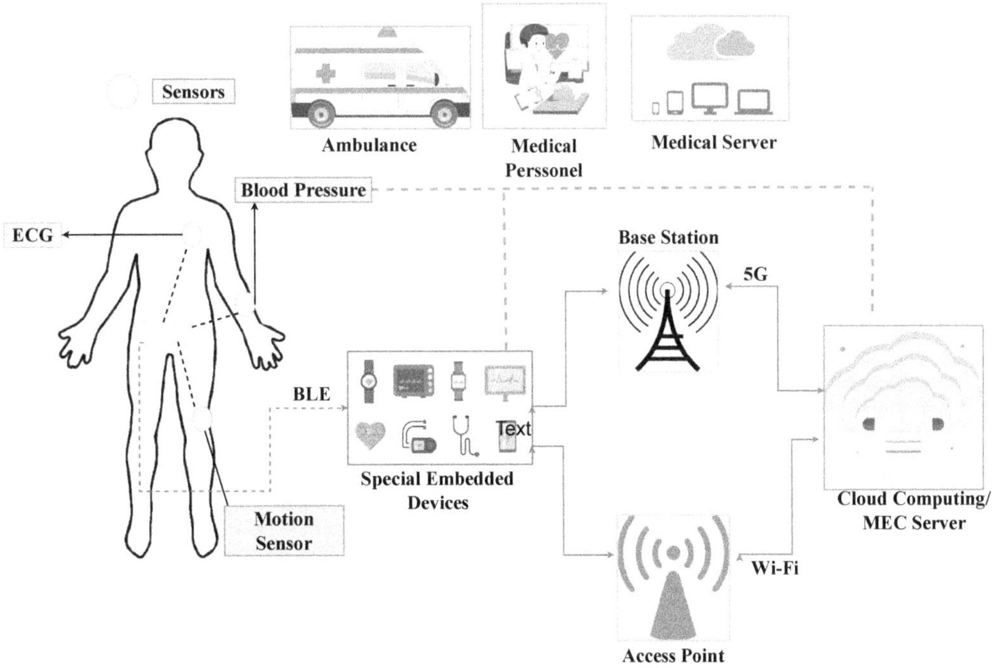

Fig. 1.4 IoMT Model for smart health control system.

1.3 Research issues in IoT

The IoT can optimize the utilization of the Internet according to the needs of its end-users. This feature must address various unresolved issues linked to the Internet of Things concept. Fig.1.5 illustrates the current challenges in IoT. These problems may be connected to the current shortcomings of IoT. Continuous improvements have been consistently implemented to address these persistent issues (Ahad et al. 2019, Han et al. 2021).

Availability: The implementation of IoT should rely on current hardware and software to ensure they can offer access and services anytime and anywhere. IoT is often mistaken for software by many people, but it is actually an application that can offer services. The hardware component is crucial and operates through various protocols like 6LoWPAN, IPv6, CoAP, RPL, etc. The entire setup is commonly perceived as a distinct entity. Therefore, end users' understanding of the relationship between hardware and software can help focus the vision more effectively.

Reliability: The primary goal of improving reliability is to boost the success rate of IoT services by enhancing its ability to deliver information. It becomes a crucial element. Therefore, a sequence of checksums must be applied to both the hardware and software components of the IoT framework. The reliability of the IoT framework is consistently challenged by system failures and security threats.

Mobility: Mobility poses a challenge for the seamless integration of IoT due to the reliance of many applications on a mobile interface. Connectivity is crucial for data

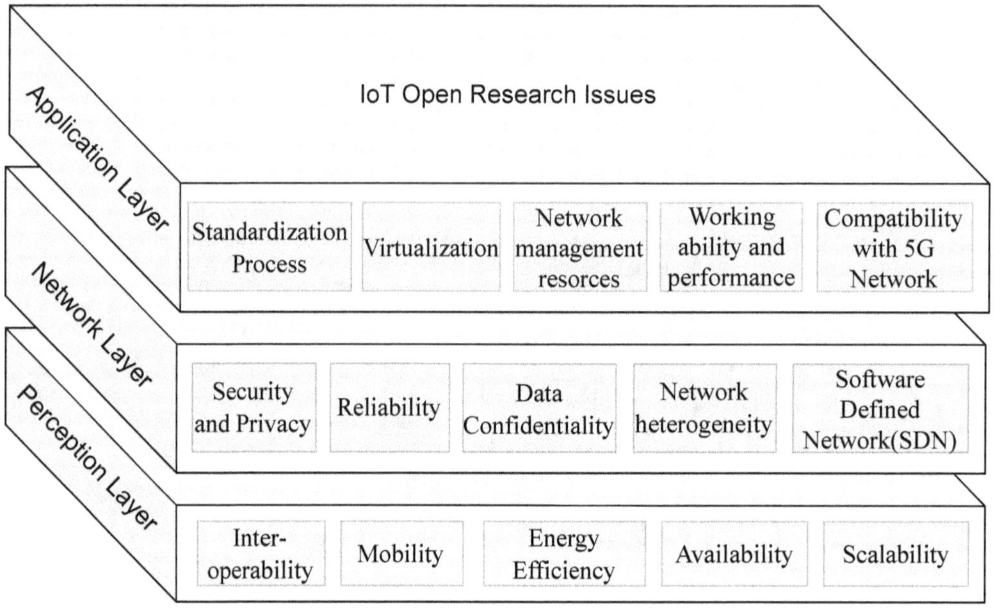

Fig. 1.5 Open research issues in IoT

mobility. Therefore, a lack of connectivity between non-stationary devices is frequently viewed as a limitation of IoT in transferring data effectively from source to destination.

Computation and Efficiency: Assessing the operational capacity and efficiency of IoT services is widely regarded as a significant challenge. Performance is closely linked to the underlying technologies, so it is essential to regularly update services to meet the needs of end-users. Another factor is the assessment of performance, which is closely linked to the cost and quality of the underlying technology. Despite the end-user's desire for optimal performance at a lower cost, evaluating the performance of any IoT application remains an unresolved issue.

Data confidentiality: Data confidentiality is a critical challenge due to the ever-changing terminologies and requirements of end-users, making it difficult to establish a stable foundation.

Resource Utilization: Connecting with a vast number of devices, the service frequently encounters challenges in managing and addressing issues such as fault configuration, ongoing performance management, and security of devices and their channels.

Scalability: It pertains to the idea of incorporating new devices into the current framework without disrupting the existing services and functionalities. Therefore, achieving collective consensus always poses a challenge in terms of scalability.

Interoperability: Managing a vast array of diverse devices can be challenging. Furthermore, challenges were encountered when trying to establish synchronization across various platforms. Therefore, interoperability is frequently a concern in relation to IoT.

Security and Privacy: Data privacy is always crucial in the context of IoT, as it involves transmitting information over the Internet. Extensive research is conducted to ensure data transmission security, though occasional shortcomings may arise.

Visualization: Many concerns arise regarding the development of a virtual alternative to address the current issues with contemporary applications. One of the major challenges encountered by IoT is the development, appropriate deployment, and adaptability to current situations.

Compatibility with 5G communication: Despite the rapid transformation of high-speed communication systems, major innovations in 5G communication techniques for IoT implementations are often hindered by common issues. Commonly encountered challenges include implementing physical layer modulation techniques, efficiently managing multiple input multiple output systems, and error control coding.

Many efforts have been made in the field of IoT. IoT still needs to mature in several aspects. Addressing these issues requires collaborative efforts from stakeholders across industries, including technology vendors, policymakers, and standards organizations. Implementing robust security measures, promoting data privacy practices, fostering interoperability standards, and investing in research and development are essential steps toward realizing the full potential of IoT while mitigating associated risks. Continual interest from academia, industries, and other related entities in the IoT field is creating higher expectations, which can sometimes result in increased challenges without fully understanding the fundamental needs and capabilities of IoT.

1.4 Problem Statement

The review of literature has provided rich information pertaining to the emergence of technologies like cloud computing and Internet of Things (IoT). It also brought the fact to the notice that there have been efforts pertaining to remote health monitoring and the possible realization with IoT integration with healthcare units.

The authors (Xu et al. 2019) proposed a privacy-preserving scheme with two blockchains to ensure that both users' health data and doctors' diagnoses cannot be tampered to avoid medical disputes. They decoupled the encrypted data and the corresponding keys to achieve flexible key management. But Consequently, they are not have addressed both the confidentiality and efficiency challenges. According to (Chen 2021) proposed a system using beacon technology to assess subject well being based on lack of movement, and automatically activates prepositioned cameras and send an alert to family members or caregivers in response to potentially high-risk activity, such as activating particular kitchen appliance. but the patient details not protected on a local server privacy and data of security.

To (Bhuiyan et al. 2021, Ghubaish et al. 2020), present state-of-the-art techniques to secure IoMT systems' data during collection, transmission, and storage. We comprehensively overview IoMT systems' potential attacks, including physical and network attacks. But it did not considered various types of attacks and framework proposed. A Telecare Medical Information System (TMIS) using Cloud Environment (CE) is proposed by (Deebak and Al-Turjman 2020). The cryptanalysis has demonstrated are susceptible to the potential attacks namely Patient Anonymity, Health-Report Revelation Health-Report Forgery, Report Confidentiality, and Non-Repudiation. This model is insecure against the patient anonymity, healthreport revelation, health-report forgery, report confidentiality, non-repudiation and fails to validate the service access. The author (Liang et al. 2021) proposed PPDT, which enables privacy-preserving decision tree classification for health monitoring systems. PPDT transforms a decision tree classifier into the Boolean vectors and utilizes symmetric encryption to protect the data privacy. Though this research addressed both the confidentiality and efficiency challenges simultaneously, it is not designed to classify against malicious adversaries.

As summary, many researcher contributed to improve, secure and enhance the remote monitoring of patients with different aspects. However, considering rural people who can reach nearby PHC need remote health monitoring, different problems found in the literature are considered. First, the problem of proposing the smart bed based remote health monitoring system associated with village PHC where patient's vital signs like temperature and heart beat (other parameters can be obtained based on the usage of wearable sensors) can be sent to cloud which is accessible to all the stakeholders of the use case including doctor through a mobile application. Second, the problem of realizing the system by exploiting technology driven innovations. Third, the problem of providing security enhancements to the proposed remote health monitoring system to have end to end security to communications besides preserving privacy.

The healthcare industry stands on the precipice of a technological revolution driven by the convergence of the IoT and blockchain technologies, coupled with the transformative capabilities of machine learning. While this convergence offers unprecedented opportunities to enhance patient care, streamline healthcare operations, and improve decision-making, it also presents a myriad of complex challenges that demand immediate attention.

Security vulnerabilities in healthcare IoT: One of the foremost challenges is the security of healthcare data in the context of IoT. The proliferation of IoT devices in healthcare, including wearable sensors, remote monitoring devices, and smart medical equipment, has created a vast attack surface susceptible to various security threats. These threats encompass data breaches, unauthorized access to patient information, interference with medical devices, and the compromise of sensitive patient data. Ensuring the confidentiality, integrity, and availability of healthcare data has become paramount.

Privacy concerns and regulatory compliance: Healthcare data is highly sensitive, encompassing not only medical histories and treatment plans but also personal and demographic information. The unauthorized exposure of such data poses serious privacy risks to patients. Additionally, healthcare providers and institutions are subject to stringent regulatory frameworks, including HIPAA and GDPR, which mandate strict adherence to data privacy and security standards. Non-compliance can lead to severe legal and financial consequences.

The Need for immutable data integrity: Data integrity is a critical concern in healthcare. The accurate recording and preservation of medical data are essential for patient safety and the reliability of medical research. Traditional centralized databases are vulnerable to data tampering, which can have life-threatening consequences in healthcare. Ensuring the immutability and authenticity of healthcare records is paramount for maintaining trust in the system.

Dynamic threat landscape: The threat landscape in healthcare is dynamic and ever-evolving. Malicious actors constantly devise new attack vectors and techniques to exploit vulnerabilities in IoT networks and healthcare systems. Traditional security measures often struggle to keep pace with these emerging threats, necessitating adaptive and innovative security solutions.

Integration challenges and scalability: Integrating blockchain and ML into existing healthcare infrastructures is a complex endeavor. Blockchain's distributed ledger and cryptographic features introduce novel complexities in terms of deployment, scalability, and interoperability. Moreover, the implementation of ML algorithms for healthcare analytics must address concerns related to data privacy and the robustness of machine learning models.

The Gap between Research and Practice: While research in healthcare security using IoT, blockchain, and ML has made significant strides, there remains a considerable gap between theoretical advancements and practical implementations. Many proposed security models and solutions have not been adequately tested and validated in real-world healthcare settings. As a result, healthcare providers and organizations face uncertainty in selecting and implementing the most suitable security measures for their specific use cases.

This thesis recognizes these pressing challenges as opportunities for groundbreaking research and innovation. It aims to bridge the gap between theoretical knowledge and practical application by addressing the intricate security concerns posed by the integration of IoT, blockchain, and ML in healthcare. Through a series of research works, this thesis endeavors to contribute to the development of robust and adaptive healthcare security solutions that safeguard patient data, uphold privacy, ensure data integrity, and mitigate emerging threats.

1.5 Research Objectives

The primary aim of this thesis is to address the multifaceted challenges posed by the integration of IoT, blockchain, and ML technologies in the context of healthcare security. To accomplish this overarching goal, the following specific research objectives have been defined:

- Evaluate and Enhance IoT Security Models: The first research objective is to comprehensively assess existing IoT security models, focusing on remote health monitoring-based IoT networks. This includes the identification of network attacks, evaluation of mitigation strategies, and the design of performance-aware data security models. The goal is to bridge the gap between theoretical security models and practical deployment considerations, with a focus on adaptability and scalability.

- Create a Lightweight Signcryption Algorithm: The second research objective is to propose a Hybrid Secure Signcryption Algorithm that enhances data security in IoMT environments, particularly in Electronic Health Record exchanges. HySSA should strike a balance between security and efficiency, ensuring minimal encryption and signature overhead while safeguarding the confidentiality and integrity of healthcare data.

- Develop a Dynamic Security Model for IoMT: The third research objective is to introduce a Hybrid Metaheuristic Model for the Internet of Medical Things (IoMT) that dynamically reconfigures blockchain-based security. This model should optimize deployment security and Quality of Service (QoS) performance in real-time scenarios. By combining Elephant Herding Optimization (EHO) and Grey Wolf Optimization (GWO), the model aims to adapt to dynamic attack scenarios and provide scalable security solutions.

- Optimize Temporal QoS in IoMT Deployments: The fourth research objective involves the development of a novel bio-inspired model to improve the temporal Quality of Service (QoS) performance of IoMT deployments. Leveraging the Mayfly Optimization (MO) Method, this model should optimize block mining performance, reduce latency, decrease energy consumption, increase throughput, and enhance overall system performance.

- Establish an IoT Secure Communication Framework: The fifth research objective is to present an IoT architecture designed for secure communication and monitoring of electrocardiogram signals independently by patients. This framework should address critical security concerns, including data integrity, confidentiality, and authenticity, in the context of IoT-based healthcare applications.

- Assess and Compare Performance Metrics: Throughout the research, a comprehensive assessment and comparison of performance metrics will be conducted. These metrics include but are not limited to computational latency, energy consumption, security levels, deployment complexity, scalability measures, attack detection and mitigation speed, throughput, and network consistency under attack scenarios. The goal is to quantitatively evaluate the effectiveness of proposed security models and algorithms.

By pursuing these research objectives, this thesis endeavors to contribute to the advancement of healthcare security in the era of IoT, blockchain, and ML. The ultimate goal is to empower healthcare providers, institutions, and researchers with innovative and adaptive security solutions that safeguard patient data, uphold privacy, and enhance the efficiency of healthcare systems.

1.6 Thesis Organization

The organization of this thesis is structured to provide a comprehensive exploration of healthcare security using Machine Learning and Blockchain technologies in the context of the IoMT. This section outlines the chapters and sub-sections that compose the thesis.

Chapter 1: Introduction This opening chapter introduces the readers to the research topic and lays the foundation for the entire study. It begins with a background and motivation for the research, followed by a clear delineation of the problem statement and research objectives. The chapter also outlines the scope and limitations of the study, emphasizing its significance in addressing pertinent issues in healthcare security. Furthermore, it provides a roadmap for the thesis by describing the organization of subsequent chapters.

Chapter 2: Literature Survey undertakes an in-depth literature survey to establish the theoretical and conceptual underpinnings of healthcare security in the context of IoMT. It delves into various aspects of healthcare security, IoT in healthcare, security models, blockchain technology, and machine learning, providing readers with a solid understanding of the existing body of knowledge. This chapter also identifies gaps and challenges in the current literature, which set the stage for subsequent research endeavors.

Chapter 3: Advances the discussion by presenting the first research work, which introduces the Hybrid Secure Signcryption Algorithm (HySSA) for securing Electronic Health Records (EHR) exchange in IoMT. Readers are guided through the phases of the algorithm's operation, emphasizing its cost-effectiveness, performance metrics, and superiority over existing schemes. This chapter underscores the significance of HySSA in addressing security concerns in IoMT.

Chapter 4: Transitions into the core of the thesis, focusing on the Second research work. It introduces the challenges in IoMT security and presents the innovative Hybrid Metaheuristic Model developed to enhance healthcare data security. Sub-sections delve into the model's components, optimization techniques, and empirical evaluation. The chapter culminates in a comparative analysis, showcasing the contributions and improvements achieved through the proposed model.

Chapter 5: Delves into the third research work, unveiling the Q-Learning Model's innovative approach to enhancing blockchain security in IoMT networks. This chapter discusses the challenges in temporal QoS performance and introduces the Mayfly Optimization (MO) Method. It systematically explores the performance metrics and comparative analysis, emphasizing the model's potential to optimize real-time healthcare deployments.

Chapter 6: The final chapter, serves as the conclusion of the thesis. It summarizes the key findings, contributions, and implications of the research. This chapter reflects on the practical implications of the thesis and offers insights into future directions for research and development in the domain of healthcare security using ML and Blockchain in IoMT. It underscores the thesis's significance in enhancing healthcare efficiency and security.

In summary, this thesis is meticulously organized to provide a cohesive and comprehensive exploration of healthcare security in the context of IoMT, with each chapter building upon the previous one to contribute to a holistic understanding of the subject matter.

CHAPTER 2

LITERATURE REVIEW

2.1 Introduction

The proverb Health is Wealth has been true for a very long time. Even though man is able to launch rockets to other planets, he still has health problems. Technology has made healthcare sophisticated, tech-rich, and able to treat many diseases. However, it became expensive, and people worldwide spend a lot on health. It appears that most people cannot afford healthcare. Thus, using technology to provide healthcare to the poor is crucial. Urban healthcare is available to those with money or insurance. What about rural residents without access to expensive medical care? Technological systems must answer this question. Technology is useless unless it helps the poor. This idea motivates academics and researchers to study computer industry innovations. The concept is based on helping remote villagers. This concept enabled remote health monitoring attempts. A few years ago, this was unthinkable. Remote health monitoring systems may be possible with cloud computing and Internet of Things technologies, which rely on distributed computing (Khan 2017).

IoT integration with applications has many benefits. The IoT can improve device-to-device communication. Thus, it enables machine-to-machine communication without human intervention. The Internet of Things will reduce machine inefficiency (Ji et al. 2019). IoT gathers data using sensor networks. Data analysis yields three informed choices. IoT enables M2M communications for automation and control. Because devices and data are easily accessible, automation and control can be more advanced. Application monitoring is easier with IoT. It can monitor effectively due to its predictive knowledge. It tracks supply chain operations, energy, water, security, supply quantity, and more. In real life, M2M response times will save time and improve system efficiency. In addition, IoT could improve people's daily lives. Everything becomes more advanced, productive, and efficient (Gull et al. 2020, Rinki et al. 2022).

To secure remote health monitoring IoT devices, models must integrate data, node, network, and route security models for multiple IoT deployments. These models must detect, stop, and neutralize internal and external attacks. Figure 2.1 shows a typical IoT security model for remote health monitoring (Ahad et al. 2019). Integration of security at the physical device level is possible for connectivity, edge computing, data accumulation, abstraction, application level, and collaboration/processing level. Security models for IoT devices and deployments include kernel, network access, communication, tamper proofing, storage, authentication, access control, and identity management.

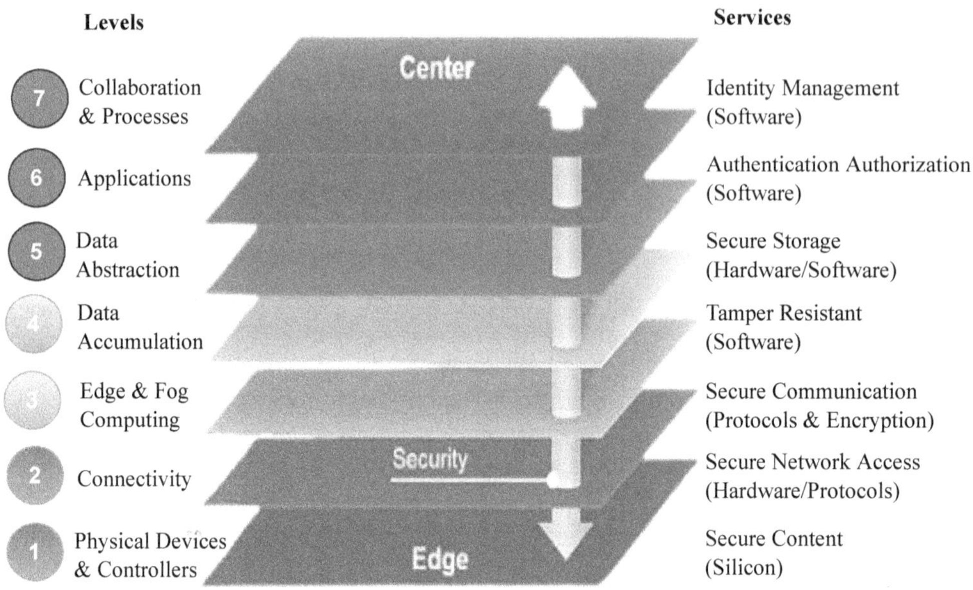

Fig. 2.1 A Typical IoT Security Model.

2.2 IoT with Machine Learning

ML involves employing intelligent techniques to enhance performance metrics by leveraging example data or past experiences through the process of learning. Specifically, ML algorithms construct behavior models using mathematical methods applied to extensive datasets. ML also facilitates learning without direct programming, enabling models to adapt and improve. These models serve as a foundation for making predictions based on new input data. ML is interdisciplinary, drawing from various fields such as artificial intelligence, optimization theory, information theory, and cognitive science (Malani et al. 2019).

ML is applied in scenarios where human expertise is either unavailable or impractical, such as navigating hazardous environments where human skills cannot be utilized effectively, as seen in robotics and speech recognition. It is also employed in situations where solutions to specific problems evolve over time, such as routing in computer networks or detecting malicious code in software applications. Additionally, machine learning is integral to practical smart systems; for example, Google utilizes ML to analyze threats against mobile endpoints and Android applications, as well as for identifying and removing malware from infected devices. Similarly, Amazon has introduced Macie, a service that employs ML to categorize and organize data stored in its cloud platform. While machine learning techniques excel in numerous domains, they may produce false positives and true negatives, necessitating guidance and model adjustments in case of inaccurate predictions. In contrast, DL, a subset of ML, allows models to evaluate prediction accuracy autonomously. Due to their self-assessment capabilities, DL models are particularly well-suited for classification and prediction tasks in cutting-edge IoT applications requiring contextual and personalized assistance.

While conventional methods are extensively employed for various facets of IoT, such as applications, services, architectures, protocols, data aggregation, resource allocation, clustering, and analytics, including security, the widespread deployment of IoT necessitates intelligent, resilient, and dependable techniques. In this regard, ML and DL emerge as promising approaches for IoT networks for several reasons. For instance, IoT networks generate vast volumes of data, which are essential inputs for ML and DL methodologies, enabling the infusion of intelligence into the systems.

Moreover, ML and DL techniques enhance the utilization of data generated by IoT, empowering IoT systems to make informed and intelligent decisions. These techniques are extensively applied in security, privacy, attack detection, and malware analysis within IoT contexts. Additionally, DL methods can be integrated into IoT devices to execute intricate sensing and recognition tasks, facilitating the development of innovative applications and services that accommodate real-time interactions among humans, smart devices, and physical environments.

However, integrating ML and DL techniques into IoT applications presents multifaceted challenges. For example, developing appropriate models capable of processing data from diverse IoT applications poses a significant hurdle. Additionally, effectively labeling input data can be a cumbersome task. Another challenge arises from the need to minimize labeled data usage in the learning process. Furthermore, deploying these models on resource-constrained IoT devices requires reducing processing and storage overheads. Similarly, critical infrastructure and real-time applications may be unable to tolerate anomalies introduced by ML or DL algorithms. Given these challenges, it becomes essential to systematically review IoT security solutions that harness ML and DL techniques. The fusion of machine learning with IoT presents substantial opportunities to augment the capabilities and effectiveness of IoT systems. Through the utilization of machine learning algorithms, IoT devices can scrutinize extensive datasets produced by sensors and actuators, extract valuable insights, and execute intelligent decisions instantaneously. This amalgamation facilitates a myriad of applications and scenarios across various industries, encompassing predictive maintenance, anomaly detection, personalized recommendations, and autonomous control (Shafiq et al. 2020).

ML algorithms play a pivotal role in uncovering patterns, trends, and correlations within IoT data, facilitating predictive analytics to foresee equipment failures, optimize resource allocation, and enhance overall system performance. Moreover, these algorithms have the capability to adapt and learn from new data, thereby refining the accuracy and efficacy of IoT solutions over time. Nevertheless, integrating machine learning with IoT presents challenges such as safeguarding data privacy, ensuring security, and managing computational resource constraints. Addressing these challenges necessitates thoughtful consideration and the implementation of appropriate measures to uphold the reliability and integrity of IoT deployments. Despite these hurdles, the symbiosis between machine learning and IoT holds immense promise to transform industries, propel innovation, and unlock new opportunities for businesses and society at large.

The integration of machine learning with IoT technologies holds the promise of transforming industries by making systems more intelligent, autonomous, and efficient. However, it also presents challenges, including data privacy concerns, the need for robust data processing infrastructures, and the development of advanced ML models that can operate effectively with the constraints of IoT devices.

2.3 IoT with Blockchain

The healthcare industry has undergone a paradigm shift in recent years due to the swift progression of technology. This shift is characterized by the revolutionary nature of the integration between blockchain technology and the Internet of Things. The convergence of these revolutionary technologies has resulted in the conception of healthcare systems that are both secure and efficient. This has enabled improved patient monitoring, timely decision-making, and the smooth transfer of vital medical information. Healthcare practitioners and scholars persistently investigate novel approaches to address the perpetual challenges of the sector. In this regard, the convergence of blockchain technology and the Internet of Things has surfaced as a promising development (Mohanta et al. 2020).

The IoT, which aims to implement 5G technologies such as smart homes and cities, e-health, and distributed intelligence, is expanding at an exponential rate each year. However, it faces security and privacy concerns. The interconnection of IoT devices follows a decentralized architecture. Thus, utilizing currently available standard security techniques to secure communication between IoT nodes is extremely difficult.

BC is a technology that ensures the confidentiality of transactions between IoT devices. It provides a publicly accessible, decentralized, and distributed shared ledger for storing the data of blocks processed and verified in an IoT network. Automatic management of the data contained in the public ledger is achieved through the utilization of the Peer-to-Peer topology. The BC is a technology in which IoT nodes exchange transactions in the form of blocks in the BC. The units are interconnected, and each device retains its prior device address. Blockchain and IoT integrate with the cloud. The BC would transform IoT communication. The advantages of integrating BC and IoT are as follows (Indumathi et al. 2020):

- Decentralized Framework: Both IoT and Blockchain (BC) employ a decentralized framework, eliminating centralized systems and enhancing the overall system's failure probability and performance.
- Security: Blockchain ensures secure transactions among nodes, offering a novel approach to secure communication. This feature extends to IoT devices, enabling them to communicate securely with each other.
- Identification: In IoT, connected devices are uniquely identified with individual IDs, mirroring the unique identification of each block in Blockchain. Thus, Blockchain serves as a trusted technology, providing uniquely identified data stored in a public ledger.
- Reliability: IoT nodes in Blockchain can authenticate information passed within the network, ensuring data reliability through verification by miners before entry into the Blockchain. Only verified blocks are allowed into the Blockchain.
- Autonomous: Within Blockchain, all IoT nodes possess the freedom to communicate with any other node in the network without reliance on a centralized system.
- Scalability: Blockchain facilitates high-availability communication among IoT devices in a distributed intelligence network, ensuring real-time information exchange with destination devices while maintaining scalability.

The blockchain technology could help solve some problems with the IoT, especially those that have to do with trust, security, and running on its own. As both technologies keep getting better, combining them should lead to big improvements and new ideas in many areas, from smart cities and healthcare to smart homes and supply lines.

2.4 Literature Review

Researchers offer several IoT security models with unique functionality for healthcare monitoring applications. The healthcare sector is rapidly shifting from a hospital- and specialist-centered paradigm to a patient-centered (Ahad et al. 2019, Han et al. 2021). The expansion of healthcare is accelerated by several technological developments. Communication technologies enable customised, remote healthcare. The 4G network and other communication technologies are used in intelligent healthcare applications today; these technologies are always changing to meet new requirements. More applications in a range of sizes and formats will produce data as the smart healthcare industry grows. Hospitals will require Massive-Machine Type Communication in order to connect a sizable number of sensor-based machines and devices as the market for smart healthcare continues to expand. Future applications like remote surgery and the tactile internet will require communications with ultra-reliability and low latency, also referred to as critical machine type communication. The current state of communication technologies is insufficient to meet the complex and dynamic requirements of intelligent healthcare applications. Fifth-generation (5G) wireless networks aim to enable intelligent healthcare applications with ultra-low latency, massive bandwidth, high reliability, high density, and remarkable energy efficiency. To increase cellular coverage, network speed, and network security, 5G and Internet of Things devices will soon be incorporated into intelligent healthcare networks. In their study, they look into taxonomy, research trends, issues, and possible future research goals in addition to intelligent healthcare made possible by 5G and the Internet of Things.

Internet of Things-connected devices are being used more and more in fields like intelligent transportation, intelligent healthcare, and smart cities, all of which generate a large amount of sensitive data. Due to the Internet of Things' widespread deployment, mobility, and performance limitations, traditional access control methods are unable to secure private data in contemporary IoT scenarios. This article explores attribute-based architecture and auditable access control. This model manages private data access control using blockchain-based request, response, and access records. A blockchain-based auditable access control (BAAC) solution is also given Fig.2.2. This solution secures personal data in Internet of Things settings and manages data efficiently and auditably. Tests show that the suggested system can maintain high throughput and data security in IoT settings.

According to (Ghorpade et al. 2021) provides an updated version of the QPSO algorithm with an emphasis on Industrial Internet of Things(IIoT) settings. As such, there is an improvement in latency, energy efficiency, and connectivity. To find the most effective ways to build different network topologies, researchers conduct investigations and hunt for solutions. It uses inputs from multiple IIoT technologies to optimise systems inspired by biology and quantum mechanics.

As per reference (Kumar et al. 2020), the decentralised data network, transparency, immutability, and crypto-security of blockchain technology render it suitable for nearly all industries. Transparency, quicker and easier access, security, efficacy, and other desired qualities are offered by a smart healthcare system that integrates blockchain data with healthcare 4.0 initiatives. The 4.0 themes include cloud, fog, edge computing, AI, IoT in healthcare, IIoT, and cognitive computing. They intend to accomplish their goal of creating a sophisticated healthcare system by fusing Blockchain 3.0 and Healthcare 4.0 (B3H4) with the current healthcare infrastructure. The accessibility analysis for

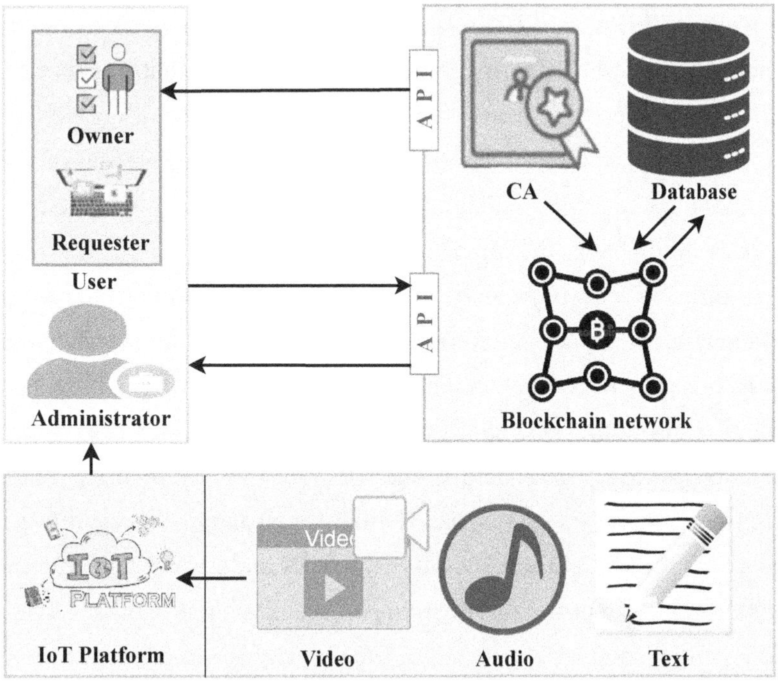

Fig. 2.2 Blockchain-based auditable access control system.

healthcare 4.0 data is carried out using techniques based on statistical simulation and optimisation. The Ethereum blockchain is built using a variety of technologies, such as web3.js, Athena, and Solidity.

The methodology, applications, needs, outcomes, and prospective future directions are the main subjects of the survey. An inventory of companies, groups, and enterprises involved in electronic health records, electronic medical records, or electronic personal records is gathered, and a comparative study is conducted on how blockchain technology has been implemented into each of their respective fields.

High levels of mobility, high data rates, high operating frequencies, and extremely low latency are all attributes of 6G technology, according to (Le et al. 2022). The advantages of 6G over 5G could contribute to the development of smart healthcare into an advanced intelligent system that can effectively address a variety of issues and concerns (such as delayed ambulance response times). Patients and providers communicate with each other through a readily accessible internet channel. The study conducted by these researchers outlines a 6G-enabled intelligent healthcare setting. Based on our investigation, the most effective and intuitive multi-server communication protocol is the Centerless User-Controlled Single Sign-On (CL-UCSSO) protocol. Three-factor authentication (password, smart card, and biometrics) combined with a time-limited feature creates a protocol that allows fast authentication and secure communication between patients and providers. This offers a rapid, safe method of connection. Using the RoR, AVISPA, and BAN lines of reasoning, it is demonstrated that the proposed protocol is secure. Performance comparisons show that our work is more affordable than comparable work from other providers while providing equivalent functionality. The integration of cloud-edge (CE) concepts with the Internet of Things (IoT) has the potential to enhance the efficiency of data collection and management for IoT nodes, as suggested in (Zhang, Li, Liu, Hu and Zheng 2021).

In order to reduce the risks and hazards associated with the installation of Internet of Things-based smart technologies and to implement appropriate management mechanisms, it is imperative that an analysis of the security of IoT-based smart environments, such as smart homes and smart cities, be conducted (Karie et al. 2021). Finding security standards and assessment frameworks that satisfy security requirements and carry out in-depth analysis of IoT-based smart environments may prove to be challenging. The authors assess current security standards and assessment frameworks, as well as a number of NIST special publications on security methodology, to analyse this gap and find potential solutions for some of the security issues associated with IoT-based smart environments.

IoT is made up of billions of intelligent devices that can communicate with each other with little help from humans, according to (Al-Garadi et al. 2020). One of the computer industries with the fastest rate of growth is the Internet of Things, with 50 billion connected devices predicted by 2020. New security challenges have been brought about by transdisciplinary components and cross-cutting IoT systems.

2.5 IoT security using Machine Learning

The vulnerabilities of Internet of Things devices cannot be addressed by encryption, authentication, access control, network security, or application security. The current security measures need to be improved in order to safeguard the IoT ecosystem. Machine learning have advanced in the last few years, and machine intelligence has moved from lab settings to important applications. IoT security is being transformed by ML strategies from a safe device connection to intelligence-based security. Their research offers a thorough analysis of ML technologies that could be applied to improve IoT security. IoT system attack surfaces and associated risks are explored, along with IoT security risks associated with new or existing threats.

2.5.1 Scope of Machine Learning in IoT Applications

Machine Learning plays a pivotal role in Internet of Things applications by harnessing data from connected devices to drive insights and automation.

Machine learning algorithms evaluate data from Internet of Things sensors to forecast equipment malfunctions, allowing for preemptive maintenance and reducing operational interruptions. Machine learning algorithms are utilized to detect anomalous patterns in Internet of Things data streams, hence aiding in the early detection of cybersecurity risks or system failures. Machine learning enhances the utilization of resources in Internet of Things systems, including energy and raw materials, thereby enhancing efficiency and minimizing waste. Machine learning customizes user experiences by utilizing data from Internet of Things devices and providing individualized services and suggestions. ML evaluates data from medical IoT devices to monitor patient health, discover anomalies, and deliver individualized treatment suggestions. Machine learning algorithms analyze environmental data collected from Internet of Things sensors in order to identify and quantify pollution levels, evaluate potential hazards, and provide assistance to conservation initiatives. Machine learning enhances manufacturing processes and supply chain activities in Internet of Things-enabled companies, resulting in improved efficiency and quality control.

Machine learning empowers independent decision-making in Internet of Things devices and cars, improving navigation, obstacle detection, and safety. Machine learning enhances energy efficiency and facilitates the integration of renewable energy sources in buildings and smart grids that are enabled with Internet of Things technology. Deploying machine learning algorithms at the edge of Internet of Things networks allows for immediate analysis and decision-making, resulting in less delay and improved responsiveness.

In order to prevent unwanted traffic flows, it is critical for the security of the Internet of Things network to identify abnormal and malicious traffic in the IoT network. To reduce harmful communication flows related to the internet of things, a large number of academics have created machine learning algorithms. When classifying hazardous traffic flows, machine learning algorithms frequently error by using incorrect features. To choose the most important characteristics for the most accurate fraud detection in IoT networks, further research is needed. building an entirely new structure in order to address the problem. After introducing a novel feature selection metric called CorrAUC, which is based on the wrapper approach, a new feature selection technique called CorrAUC is introduced. This technique uses the area under the curve (AUC) metric to accurately filter features and select useful features for the chosen machine learning algorithm. This is carried out in an effort to raise the ML algorithm's accuracy. CorrAUC was developed and designed with inspiration from the wrapper method. This made it possible for them to evaluate the system's effectiveness. Utilizing data from Bot-IoT in combination with four distinct machine learning algorithms, researchers test our approaches. The results of the experiments showed that our suggested strategy could potentially achieve over 96% success in various scenarios. Federated learning, is gaining traction as a method for facilitating IoMT data interoperability while protecting user privacy (Malani et al. 2019, Shafiq et al. 2020).

2.5.2 Security solutions using Machine learning

The field of machine learning-based security solutions for IoT devices has evolved in recent years, and experts want to contribute to it. This section discusses machine learning methods for IoT system security. These methods have been examined using the three main architectural levels of an IoT system: physical/perception, network, and web/application.

Physical/Perception Layer: Conventional authentication methods utilized for surface protection often fall short in detecting precise cutoff values required to distinguish unwanted signals, leading to false alarms (Xiao et al. 2016). Machine learning-based approaches offer an alternative to traditional password verification at the physical layer. According to (Xiao et al. 2016), employing Q-learning-based methods reduces authentication errors by 64.3% and outperforms conventional physical layer authentication techniques, particularly with 12 emitters. In another study, supervised ML techniques such as distributed Frank-Wolfe and incremental aggregated gradient were utilized to optimize parameters in a logistics regression model, aiming to reduce communication costs and enhance the accuracy of fake detection (Xiao, Wan and Han 2017). Additionally, unsupervised learning methods like IGMM are employed to safeguard surfaces and ensure the authenticity of IoT devices (Xiao, Wan and Han 2017).

To ensure the security of the Internet of Things, research in (Wang et al. 2017, Shi et al. 2017, Namvar et al. 2016) has demonstrated that Reinforcement Learning (RL) approaches are effective in mitigating jamming attacks. In (Namvar et al. 2016), a centralized system design was investigated for addressing aggressive jamming attacks. To combat such attacks, an intelligent power distribution method and an IoT access point were employed. Another study (Han et al. 2017) integrated RL with deep Convolutional Neural Networks (CNNs) to prevent signal jamming in cognitive radios, thereby enhancing RL performance. Cognitive radio (CR) devices possess dynamic capabilities that adapt to varying work situations (Bkassiny et al. 2012).

A recent proposal in (Balthar et al. 2018) introduced a novel centralized scheme based on machine learning to enhance the security of IoT devices. This scheme authorizes users to communicate with the system securely, storing their information securely as well. In the suggested peer-to-peer security protocol, users are required to register with the cloud server before initiating communication within the IoT system. Additionally, (Alam et al. 2018) introduced a model utilizing a neural network (NN) and the ElGamal algorithm to secure IoT devices and thwart potential attacks. This model utilizes private and public keys to manage its cryptosystem. Manipulated data is segmented into categories and compared to training data to ensure security. Moreover, (Baracaldo et al. 2018) presents an innovative defense strategy that identifies and filters harmful data used to train a supervised learning model.

Network Layer: Securing network layers poses challenges as cyber attacks become increasingly prevalent, bridging the gap between virtual and physical realms. In response, various supervised machine learning algorithms such as Support Vector Machines (SVM), Neural Networks (NN), and K-Nearest Neighbors (K-NN) are deployed for intrusion attack detection (Buczak and Guven 2015, Branch et al. 2013, Diro and Chilamkurti 2018). For instance, (Kulkarni and Venayagamoorthy 2009) utilized NN to detect denial-of-service threats in IoT networks through a multilayer perception-based control mechanism. Similarly, (Saied et al. 2016) proposed an Artificial Neural Network (ANN) model for detecting Distributed Denial-of-Service (DDoS) attacks, ensuring that only legitimate data packets are permitted to pass through the network. Continuously training ANN with updated datasets was identified as crucial for enhancing its performance in detecting DDoS attacks. Furthermore, findings from (Yu et al. 2008) indicate that an SVM-based ML approach in IoT systems achieved a remarkable attack detection rate of 99.4 percent.

In their work, (Miettinen et al. 2017) introduced the IoT SENTINEL model, which utilizes a Random Forest (RF) method to classify IoT devices into groups. This classification aids in protecting them from potential threats arising from unsecured device connections, thereby safeguarding them against damage. Similarly, (Meidan et al. 2017) employed machine learning classifier methods to categorize IoT devices, distinguishing them from non-IoT devices within a network. By partitioning devices into these two groups, the classifier effectively manages connections for non-IoT devices and mitigates potential threats. Additionally, an earlier study by (Lee et al. 2017) investigated the impact of anomalous behavior exhibited by IoT devices on the detection accuracy of machine learning algorithms such as Support Vector Machines (SVM) and K-Means. They observed a decrease in accuracy when training datasets were altered, highlighting the need for further research to understand the factors influencing variations in accuracy and training data composition.

In safeguarding Internet of Things devices, (Nobakht et al. 2016) proposed a network-layer intrusion detection method utilizing machine learning (ML) algorithms. Due to dataset imbalance, the classifier's performance was assessed using recall, accuracy, and precision metrics. However, employing performance metrics based on the area under the receiver operating characteristic curve (AUC) may yield more robust results (Bradley 1997, He and Garcia 2009). Similarly, (Suarez et al. 2016) utilized Artificial Neural Network (ANN) methods to train computers in identifying anomalies within IoT networks. While initial experimental results were promising, further research is needed to evaluate the system's efficacy with larger datasets prone to increased data manipulation attempts. Additionally, (Wold et al. 1987) employed unsupervised machine learning techniques, combining c-means clustering and principal component analysis, to develop an Intrusion Detection System (IDS) capable of identifying more IoT-related threats. Another study implemented an intrusion detection framework for IoT networks using an unsupervised ML technique known as optimal-path forest (Rocha et al. 2009, Dean and Ghemawat 2008).

In 2018, (Doshi et al. 2018) proposed a technique for detecting local IoT device DDoS attacks, utilizing flow-based and protocol-agnostic traffic data along with low-cost machine learning methods. This model accounts for specific behaviors observed in restricted IoT networks, such as endpoint computation and time intervals between packets. Various classifiers were evaluated for attack detection, including K-Nearest Neighbors (KNN), the KDTree algorithm, Support Vector Machine (SVM) with linear kernel (LSVM), Decision Trees (DT) with Gini impurity scores, Random Forest (RF) with Gini impurity scores, and Neural Networks (NN). The proposed methods successfully identify distributed denial of service (DDoS) attacks on local IoT devices via home gateway routers and other intermediary network devices. Test set accuracy exceeds 0.99 for all five tested methods. Some of the important existing methods which uses ML algorithms for security in IoT is summarized in table 2.1.

Web/Application Layer: ML methods including K-NN, RF, Q-learning, and Dyna-Q have been widely used to safeguard IoT devices from web and application risks, including malware detection (Xiao, Li, Huang and Du 2017, Narudin et al. 2016). Researchers (Narudin et al. 2016) discovered that RF methods enhanced MalGenome dataset detection rates compared to K-NN, a supervised ML algorithm. Q-learning surpasses Dyna-Q-based detection learning in latency and accuracy (Xiao, Li, Huang and Du 2017).

2.5.3 Limitations of Machine Learning in IoT Applications

The integration of machine learning with Internet of Things applications brings forth numerous opportunities for innovation, yet it also presents several inherent limitations and hurdles. One of the primary challenges lies in the resource constraints of many IoT devices. These devices often possess limited computational power, memory, and energy resources, making it arduous to deploy resource-intensive ML algorithms on them effectively.

Furthermore, the implementation of ML algorithms in IoT environments raises significant concerns regarding data privacy and security. Transmitting raw data to centralized ML models for processing poses potential risks of data breaches and privacy violations, necessitating careful consideration and robust security measures.

Moreover, the nature of IoT data adds another layer of complexity. Data generated by IoT devices tends to be noisy, incomplete, and prone to inconsistencies, demanding extensive preprocessing efforts to render it suitable for ML applications. This preprocessing stage can be computationally intensive and may strain the limited resources of

Table 2.1 Machine learning based security solutions

Author	Advantages	Limitations
(Anjum et al. 2022)	Provides a comprehensive analysis of a wide range of IoT technologies that can be used in diagnosing and monitoring COVID-19 infected individuals and hotspot areas.	The wearable devices in terms of accuracy and comfortability are acknowledged, but no specific solutions or alternatives are proposed.
(Ismail et al. 2020)	The model uses intelligent data retrieval and classification techniques to study disease and predict abnormal health conditions, providing personalized healthcare and disease prevention services.	The experimental results of the proposed model are compared with three different machine learning techniques, but there is no comparison with other state-of-the-art models, which limits the evaluation of its performance.
(Hady et al. 2020)	The authors propose a real-time Enhanced Healthcare Monitoring System (EHMS) testbed that combines network flow metrics and biometric data for intrusion detection	Certain machine learning methods may not be suitable for health monitoring systems
(More et al. 2020)	The study optimizes computational time, leading to increased efficiency in processing medical images	The author does not provide security with IoT devices and servers
(Tahsien et al. 2020)	The paper Describes the potential benefits of using ML algorithms in detecting new attacks and providing security protocols for IoT devices	The paper does not address the challenges and limitations specific to the implementation and deployment of ML algorithms in IoT systems, such as computational restrictions and energy consumption
(Ahmad and Alsmadi 2021)	The paper presents flow diagrams of multiple deep-learning models used in IoT security, providing visual representation of the models	The paper does not address the challenges an efficient, scalable, robust, and accurate intrusion detection system for IoT devices against large-scale attacks.
(Bharati and Podder 2022)	Provides an extensive analysis of machine learning (ML) systems and state-of-the-art developments in deep learning (DL) methods for enhancing IoT device protection methods	The paper does not provide specific solutions or discussions on how to ensure security or privacy in IoT systems, focusing more on suggesting privacy and security-preserving methods using DL or ML algorithms.
(Islam et al. 2021)	Comprehensive evaluation of various machine learning models (shallow and deep) for intrusion detection in IoT networks	The paper does not provide a detailed analysis of the computational requirements and scalability.

IoT devices.

In addition to data quality concerns, the real-time processing requirements of many IoT applications pose challenges for traditional ML algorithms. Achieving low-latency processing, especially on resource-constrained devices, remains a significant obstacle that needs to be addressed for the seamless integration of ML and IoT.

Interpretability and explainability are also critical considerations, particularly in domains such as healthcare and autonomous vehicles. While ML models offer remarkable predictive capabilities, their inherent complexity often renders them "black boxes," making it challenging to interpret their decisions. Ensuring transparency and interpretability is paramount, especially in scenarios where understanding the rationale behind ML-driven decisions is crucial.

Furthermore, the dynamic nature of IoT environments presents challenges in maintaining the performance of ML models over time. Data distributions and relationships may evolve, necessitating continuous model adaptation and retraining to sustain optimal performance—a task that can be particularly daunting in resource-constrained IoT settings.

Managing and updating ML models deployed across a myriad of IoT devices is yet another significant challenge. Ensuring scalability, reliability, and compliance with regulatory requirements such as GDPR and HIPAA further complicate the deployment and maintenance of ML-powered IoT systems.

In conclusion, addressing these challenges requires concerted efforts from interdisciplinary teams comprising experts in machine learning, IoT system design, cybersecurity, data privacy, and domain-specific knowledge. Through collaborative endeavors and innovative approaches, researchers and practitioners strive to overcome these limitations and unlock the full potential of ML in IoT applications.

2.6 IoT security using Blockchain

Working on IoT security using blockchain involves leveraging the inherent security features of blockchain technology to enhance the security and trustworthiness of IoT systems. One of the primary ways blockchain can contribute to IoT security is through the establishment of a decentralized and tamper-resistant ledger for recording IoT device transactions and interactions. By recording each transaction in a block that is linked to previous blocks in a chronological and immutable manner, blockchain ensures that the data exchanged between IoT devices remains secure and tamper-proof.

Additionally, blockchain can be used to implement robust authentication and access control mechanisms for IoT devices. Through the use of cryptographic keys and smart contracts, blockchain enables secure and automated verification of device identities and permissions, ensuring that only authorized devices can access sensitive data and resources within the IoT network.

Moreover, blockchain can enhance the resilience of IoT networks against various cyber threats, including DDoS attacks and data breaches. The decentralized nature of blockchain ensures that there is no single point of failure, making it more difficult for malicious actors to compromise the security of IoT systems.

In summary, working on IoT security using blockchain involves leveraging the unique features of blockchain technology, such as decentralization, immutability, and cryptographic security, to enhance the security, trustworthiness, and resilience of IoT systems. By integrating blockchain into IoT deployments, organizations can mitigate cybersecurity risks, protect sensitive data, and build more secure and trustworthy IoT ecosystems.

2.6.1 Scope of Blockchain in IoT applications

The Internet of Things is the technology that has grown the fastest over the past ten years due to the sharp rise in smart device and related technology from both industry and research perspectives. Applications for real-time monitoring use IoT. Due to their low processing and storage capacities, as well as the shortcomings of current security and cryptography techniques, smart objects are susceptible to attacks. Vulnerabilities in IoT security and privacy are found in the analysis. Second, blockchain-based security solutions are proposed by researchers. IoT integration and enabling technologies are included in the explanations. An Ethereum-based blockchain is integrated into an intelligent Internet of Things system, and the outcomes are examined for immediate applications (Mohanta et al. 2020).

The Internet of Medical Things powered by blockchain is becoming more and more popular in the healthcare sector, according to extensions in (Jolfaei et al. 2021), since it lowers healthcare costs while enhancing treatment quality through real-time, continuous monitoring. IoT wearable medical devices, IoMT sensor nodes, patients, healthcare facilities, and insurance companies are all gradually included in IoMT systems. Designing scalable blockchain architectures is therefore difficult. An investigation into blockchain-IoMT systems was carried out by researchers in reaction to this discovery. There is a difference in scalability between these systems based on comparisons and analysis.

According to (Iqbal et al. 2020), the Internet of Things is allegedly transforming people's lives by controlling and keeping an eye on smart objects. Smart cities, housing, automobiles, manufacturing, electronic healthcare, intelligent control systems, wearables, transportation, and farming are just a few industries that have adopted IoT applications. The need to gather and evaluate more data is increasing as these devices are used by more people. Numerous security issues and vulnerabilities can affect these devices. This discourages consumers from using them in delicate situations, like e-health, smart homes, etc., and could be detrimental to the Internet of Things future growth.

According to (Garg et al. 2020), the Internet of Medical Things is a networked infrastructure made up of software applications, health systems, intelligent medical equipment, and services. Many of the medical devices and apps have built-in internet connectivity. Machine-to-machine communication and cloud data storage are made feasible by Wi-Fi enabled devices. Compared to conventional methods, IoMT provides accurate diagnosis at a lower cost and with fewer errors. With smartphone apps enabling the IoMT, patients can share personal health information with their physicians. This enhances the monitoring, prevention, and management of illness. IoMT organisations' insecure communication may allow a hostile actor to obtain sensitive health information. An enemy may, for example, intercept, alter, remove, or add such messages while they are being transmitted. Healthcare data stored in the cloud is securely accessible to users who have successfully authenticated. All medical data is kept on cloud-hosted servers via the blockchain. Automated Validation of Internet Security Protocols and Applications (AVISPA) is the programme used to perform BAKMP-security validation of IoMT's resilience to possible attacks. It is demonstrated that BAKMP-IoMT provides enhanced security and functionality at a lower cost of processing and communication when compared to alternative approaches. Lastly, a simulation is run to determine how BAKMP affects the IoMT performance metrics (Whaiduzzaman et al. 2021).

2.6.2 Security solutions using Blockchain

Because Blockchain Technology employs the most recent encryptions, (Indumathi et al. 2020) recommends using it as a solution to IoMT's security problems. This framework uses blockchain technology's cost savings, speed, automation, immutability, almost impossible data loss, permanence, elimination of middlemen, decentralization of consensus, legal access to health data, data storage, accrual-based reimbursement mechanisms, and efficient supply chain management. In terms of enabling secure audits, the results of layered architecture have been demonstrated and verified to be better than the performance of previous designs. Although blockchain technology is still in its early stages of development, it is imperative that healthcare professionals are aware of its potential impact on patient-centered care.

According to the system evaluation and security analysis, performance increases are possible with lightweight access control with low network latency, high security, and high data privacy. One feasible option for giving IoT devices access to dispersed cloud services is edge computing (Nguyen et al. 2019, Pyoung and Baek 2019). A summary of blockchain based security solutions has been presented in Table 2.2. According to a recent study, blockchain technology may be used for Internet of Things device access control and decentralised data administration. Because edge servers must process a vast amount of data and transactions, they will not be able to store the entire blockchain. A lightweight and scalable blockchain known as LiTiChain. Blocks that have expired in LiTiChain can be securely removed from the chain in a manner that complies with the protocol.

The technology underlying blockchains is remarkable in its ability to evolve with the information era, claims (Singh et al. 2021). The Internet of Things may make use of blockchain technology. Distributed systems have been strengthened in a number of domains by the Internet of Things. Managing network data and transactions requires a decentralised system, which is required by blockchain technology. They explore blockchain, relevant properties, potential security threats, and efficient solutions in their study. Their research focuses on foundational concepts that could be incorporated into the architecture of blockchain systems and on security fixes that can allay concerns regarding the security of data. The essay talks about the obstacles that still need to be removed and possible directions for further research on blockchain technology and the internet of things. Due to the high processing and storage requirements, the great majority of Internet of Things devices are unable to function as blockchain nodes (Sun et al. 2021).

Because of this, blockchains are frequently stored on a single delegate node, which could be the cloud or an edge device. Three issues with this configuration are as follows: (1) When there are few delegate notes, the delegate node fails. (2) Confidential information may be exposed if the delegate node replicates blockchain data. (3) Distributed denial of service attacks can affect the delegate node. To get around these issues. According to the study's authors, an identity-based signature (IBS), attribute-based access control (ABAC) can all be combined to create a blockchain-based access control system for Internet of Things devices. There have reportedly been an increasing number of applications using the Internet of Things in recent years (Yang et al. 2021).

Ensuring the authenticity of devices is a challenge posed by the Internet of Things, as it is crucial to instilling consumer trust in the decisions they make. Device security and privacy must be guaranteed, especially in light of the IoT system's heterogeneity and the devices' constrained resource availability. For their study, the researchers created a blockchain-based authentication technique that is employed by the system. The authentication mechanism we have presented combines the power of modular square root with blockchain technology. Researchers perform a security analysis and extensive testing to demonstrate the system's utility and safety.

According to (Wang et al. 2019) Concerns about patients' right to privacy and the accuracy of their medical records are reportedly slowing down the adoption of mobile cloud computing (MCC) in the healthcare sector. Such obstacles require prompt care in order to optimize the advantages of their use. Preserve the privacy of health information

Table 2.2 Blockchain based security solutions

Author	Advantages	Limitations
(Saxena and Rao 2023)	The use of a blockchain module ensures secure transmission of patients' health data between medical facilities, enhancing privacy and security	The accessibility and reliability of the Internet connection may impact the system's response time and accuracy in determining security threats in the internet connection
(Zaabar et al. 2021)	The paper proposes a blockchain-based architecture for remote patient monitoring systems, which ensures highly assured levels of security and privacy for patient medical data.	The paper does not discuss the potential scalability issues that may arise when integrating blockchain technology with remote patient monitoring systems.
(Ramzan et al. 2022)	Evaluates medical care technologies and relevant applications based on blockchain technology.	The paper does not focus on the Security of data.
(Samuel et al. 2022)	Integrates garlic routing and blockchain to ensure low-latency communication, privacy, anonymity, trust, and security.	The simulation results presented in the paper may not fully capture the real-world complexities and dynamics of a large-scale e-health monitoring system.
(Jolfaei et al. 2021)	Discusses various approaches, including on-chain and off-chain techniques, to improve the scalability of blockchain technology in IoMT systems .	The paper does not provide the specific limitations of blockchain-based IoMT systems in terms of security and privacy concerns
(Elhachmi and Kobbane 2022)	Greater security in Data management and Resistance to cyber-attacks	Research focus on improving the efficiency, scalability, and interoperability but not on reliability
(Yin et al. 2022)	Strong protection to the original templates and effectively prevents privacy breaches in unprotected IoT applications.	Applicability of the method to other biometric authentication systems beyond fingerprint authentication
(Sabrina et al. 2022)	Introduces a lightweight time-based identification protocol (LiTBIP) for securing small IoT devices.	The evaluation of system is based on the initial prototype implementation, and it's unclear how it would perform in real-world
(Dorri et al. 2017)	Provides a lightweight instantiation of a blockchain (BC) specifically designed for IoT, eliminating the need for Proof of Work (POW) and coins.	The paper focuses on a specific use case of a smart home, and it may not directly address the security and privacy challenges in other IoT contexts.

at the local, regional, and global levels. Use security precautions when utilizing health services to keep yourself safe from hacks and vulnerabilities. With the use of management information systems (MES) and layered security models. Ensuring the security and usability of healthcare software is the aim of continuous research in the information security field (Shabbir et al. 2021). This study aims to evaluate the security and usability of software used in healthcare environments. The paper presents these empirical findings and then offers some recommendations for designing healthcare software with the highest levels of security and usability. Decision-makers aim to strike a balance between the utility and security of software when developing it.

The first step to realizing the full potential of blockchain technology is to understand the security threats and limits it presents (Hussain et al. 2020). Threat actors will take advantage of these risks and weaknesses to harm crucial resources and services. In this paper, the examiner two of the most serious blockchain security vulnerabilities: Double-spending and Sybil, using a security risk management (SRM) domain model. The framework shows the assets that are secured or will be protected, the risks associated with double-spending, the threats that an attacker may pose with a Sybil attack, the vulnerabilities of those assets, and the solutions that are appropriate for those flaws. We looked into the potential risks presented by Sybil attacks and double spending in Ethereum-based healthcare apps. Researchers are aware that blockchains' operational and security flaws preclude the technology from being widely used. Researchers look at industry-level companies' use of permissioned blockchain systems and how challenges are resolved.

2.6.3 Limitations of blockchain based models

The blockchain technology offers promising solutions for enhancing IoT security, it also presents certain limitations and challenges that need to be addressed. One key limitation is the scalability of blockchain networks, which can hinder their ability to handle the vast volume of transactions generated by IoT devices. The consensus mechanisms used in blockchain, such as proof of work or proof of stake, may lead to slower transaction processing times and higher latency, which could impact the real-time nature of many IoT applications. Moreover, the resource-intensive nature of blockchain, particularly in terms of computation and storage requirements, may pose challenges for resource-constrained IoT devices with limited processing power and memory. Implementing blockchain on such devices may lead to increased energy consumption and operational costs, which could outweigh the benefits of enhanced security.

Their findings could be useful to blockchain developers, practitioners, and other stakeholders when discussing security fixes for issues like double-spending and Sybil, as well as implementation-related limitations in blockchain systems. It is difficult for traditional centralized access control systems to permit access control in a large-scale Internet of Things environment due to mobility, poor performance, and distributed deployment. According to (Iqbal and Matulevičius 2021), the authors of the paper propose fabric-iot, a blockchain-based Internet of Things access management system, as a remedy for these issues. The Device Contract (DC), Policy Contract (PC), and Access Contract (AC) are the three distinct contracts that make up the system. DC saves and searches the URLs of device resources. PC upholds the administrator's ABAC rules. AC implements conventional user access control. Fabric-iot may be able to use blockchain and ABAC to provide decentralized, granular, and dynamic Internet of Things access control. We will create two simulation groups in order to accurately analyze this system's functionality.

The Internet of Medical Things, is fast taking center stage in remote health monitoring as a result of the growth of medical wireless sensors and advancements in communication technology (Liu, Han and Li 2020, Azeem et al. 2021). Healthcare solutions based on the internet of things are used in medical facilities to continuously observe patients. Intelligent medical devices can only handle a limited amount of data. Data security, interoperability, privacy, and anonymity are some of the issues facing the IoMT. One challenge in data aggregation and transfer is protecting patients' privacy and the confidentiality of their medical information.

It is challenging to preserve the privacy of medical photos, according to (Wang, Ali, Nazir and Niazi 2020). Medical imaging has been successfully obtained for numerous studies. By using encryption, image confidentiality is guaranteed without any data loss. Because of the enormous volume, redundancy, and capacity of e-health data, traditional encryption techniques are challenging to use. This is especially true when sending patient data over unencrypted networks. Variations in terminology and imagery regarding data loss and confidentiality put patients at risk of having their privacy violated. The security level and execution time of the proposed method are assessed and compared with those of conventional encrypted techniques. We assessed the performance of the suggested technique using a range of test photos. Several pieces of evidence suggest that the method suggested for a picture cryptosystem is the best one. The authors of the publication (Hasan et al. 2021) provide a more secure and efficient solution for HW-BAN by utilizing fewer processes, elliptic curve cryptography (ECC) and physically unclonable functions (PUF). Researchers are now able to give patients the chance to use mobile devices to check their health status in real time.

Mobile devices with integrated sensors for environmental sensing and data collection, as mentioned in (Nguyen, Leyva-Mayorga, Lewis and Popovski 2021), can enable cost-effective data interchange. Determining whether or not national and international regulations are being followed is one potential use for this data. The current IoT data exchange is unsafe and inefficient because it relies on a centralized third party because it occurs between providers and customers. Distributed ledger technology (DLT), is a technology that allows data exchange to occur while maintaining confidentiality, security, and trust. Due to a lack of knowledge regarding the effectiveness of communication between buyers and sellers, data exchange processes in Internet of Things environments are challenging to measure. Using NB-IoT technology, researchers propose a DLT-based Internet of Things data trading strategy to make widespread environmental sensing more feasible. The researchers look into the energy usage of three distinct DLT-based IoT data exchange protocols as well as the NB-IoT latency. The creation and evaluation of these protocols is the foundation for data exchange pertaining to the Internet of Things. Researchers demonstrate how network edge security measures can be implemented more easily with network function virtualization (NFV).

An electronic medical record (EMR) data-sharing system that facilitates storage, access, and exchange is called the Blockchain-Based Healthcare System (HS-BC). Additionally, this system provides patients with efficient and timely medical diagnosis and treatment. HS-BC is apprehensive about security and privacy due to blockchain technology's open nature. To give HS-BC users more privacy protection, researchers propose an attribute-based signature system that allows users to revoke attributes. By merging the attribute update-key and the attribute master-key, the user creates the attribute signing key. Whereas the attribute update-key is connected to attribute revocation, the attribute master-key is linked to the user's identity and attribute set. By merging the attribute update-key and the attribute master-key, the user creates the attribute signing key. It is feasible to revoke attributes by utilising KUNodes. The attribute-based signature technique works without a single controlling body and only needs a small number of pair keys. An extensive security analysis has demonstrated that the proposed system is unforgeable, resistant to collusion, and privacy-protecting. Researchers are examining the overall performance and storage capacity of the attribute-based signature method. Both experimental and comparative data point to its possibility. Internet of Things (IoT) devices can be found in transportation, healthcare, smart homes, smart cities, and smart grid systems (Su et al. 2020, Liao et al. 2020).

Mobile health (mHealth) and ubiquitous health (uHealth) systems give patients portable devices with embedded sensors for the delivery of healthcare services, according to research published in (Iwaya et al. 2020). It will take care of data security and privacy issues before mHealth and uHealth technologies are widely adopted. The security and privacy of m/uHealth research currently focuses on a few control families (that comply with NIST800-53), system and information protection, access control, authentication, personal involvement, and privacy authorization. These areas are underrepresented, even though the majority of users of the m/uHealth system prioritise data governance, security and privacy laws, and programme management. There is a lack of practical mHealth security and privacy review as evidenced by the overwhelming majority of studies that present novel ideas with little to no validation. It is possible that practitioners will cease implementing solutions from the literature as a result of the growing empirical research, development, and validation of m/uHealth security and privacy. Information can be shared via this SMS, giving practitioners and researchers the chance to enhance security and m/privacy uHealth. The greatest approach to address the global health issues brought on by rising healthcare costs and demand is thought to be through technological solutions, such as ubiquitous healthcare (Sun et al. 2019).

2.7 IoT security using Cryptography Algorithms

IoT security heavily relies on cryptography algorithms to safeguard data and communications within IoT systems. These algorithms play critical roles in ensuring the confidentiality, integrity, and authentication of information exchanged between IoT devices and networks. Data encryption, facilitated by algorithms like AES and RSA, ensures that sensitive data remains unreadable to unauthorised parties even if intercepted. Authentication processes, implemented using algorithms such as ECDSA and HMAC, verify the identity of IoT devices, allowing only authorised access to the network. Additionally, cryptographic hash functions like SHA-256 are used to verify data integrity by calculating message digests for transmitted data. Key management protocols ensure the secure generation, distribution, and storage of cryptographic keys, minimising the risk of key compromise. Secure communication protocols like TLS and DTLS leverage cryptographic algorithms to establish secure connections between IoT devices and servers, protecting against eavesdropping and tampering. Overall, cryptography algorithms are essential components of IoT security, providing the necessary mechanisms to safeguard IoT ecosystems against various cyber threats and ensure the integrity and privacy of IoT deployments.

2.7.1 Scope of Cryptography algorithms in IoT Applications

Many research methodologies were discussed the same issue, and collected those findings. Within a restricted Internet of Things ecosystem, we use BC to describe strategies that ensure secure data transmission between various sensors. For instance, (Mohanty et al. 2020) presented a method that, with the assistance of BC, safeguards the privacy of the data that is transferred between the sensors that make up the Internet of Things. Because BC demands a great deal of computational power, the authors concentrated on developing integrated models that are both lightweight and capable of meeting all of the IoT's requirements. (Dorri et al. 2019) suggested a lightweight, scalable BC designed for CPS ecosystem operations. The plan establishes an overlay network in which BC collectively manages high-computing devices and the throughput is determined by analyzing loads of pending transactions. However, there is little consideration given to the issue of data privacy when the sensors share information.

In the Internet of Things (IoMT) context, (Garg et al. 2020) developed a blockchain-enabled authentication key agreement protocol that provided the safe transfer of patient-centric medical information. Their solution prohibited intruders from accessing or altering the data without authorization. Furthermore, to improve security and defend against various potential threats, they employed Blockchain to store the data on the cloud server. To protect data privacy in IoMT, Ano and Canavate-Sanchez suggested a dual signature-based Elliptic Curve Digital Signature Algorithm (ECDSA) (Cano and Cañavate-Sanchez 2020).

According to (Das et al. 2019) suggested a certificate-based, lightweight access control and key agreement mechanism for IoT communication. They created a secure device access control and key agreement mechanism to safeguard the IoT communication messages. According to (Christo et al. 2021) concentrated on developing the elliptic curve cryptography (ECC) methodology, a lightweight authentication method for successfully sharing data. This study is one of numerous that have investigated wireless data sharing; it involves the storage of healthcare data on an Electronic Medical Card (EMC). The research focuses on data secrecy and data authentication, two crucial components of data security. To keep data secure, the proposed system encrypts and decrypts it using a 512-bit key using a safe technique.

To (Challa et al. 2018) created two authentication mechanisms for cloud-based CPS. Here are the protocols: 1) user and cloud server; and 2) IoT-enabled smart meter and cloud server. However, their protocols do not guarantee anonymity or untraceability. For constrained resource access, (Lara et al. 2020) presented an alternative authentication technique for industrial IoT devices. Despite being lightweight, their approach does not offer anonymity or untraceability. Additionally, their plan does not allow adding dynamic Internet of Things smart devices after deployment. The paper (Jiang et al. 2020) developed a secure three-factor authentication system for cloud and self-driving cars, utilizing passwords, smart cards, and biometrics. Blockchain technology has been used in several applications to enhance system security (Bera et al. 2020).

2.7.2 IoT security solutions using cryptography algorithms

SCBAS-SF (Vangala et al. 2021) created a revolutionary, innovative contract-based blockchain that anticipates an authenticated vital agreement mechanism in an intelligent farming scenario. The authentication stages of device-to-device (D2D) and device-to-gateway (D2G) enable mutual authentication and key agreement between two Internet of Things-enabled devices, as well as between an IoT device and the network's gateway node (GWN). Edge servers construct the blocks using authenticated data from IoT devices provided to the cloud server (CS) through GWNs. A peer-to-peer (P2P) CS network may use the intelligent contract-based consensus method to validate and add the produced blocks. However, the contract-based consensus process at each node in this architecture increases the computational burden at the edge servers, and the delay in intruder identification has not been considered.

BSKMP (Das et al. 2021) conducted thorough security research and verification. This model shows that the suggested technique resists ICPS attacks. The MIRACL multi-precision integer and rational arithmetic cryptography package was used for test-bed tests. This model's encryption method is unsuitable for data interchange security and anonymity. Participants in the peer-to-peer (P2P) network build blocks from securely received data from their SMs and add them to the blockchain after validation using a voting-based consensus procedure.

According to DBACP (Bera et al. 2020), blockchain is considered private because smart meter users provide sensitive information. This approach has better security and lower communication and computation costs than previous schemes, but the computational time for the different number of block additions and transactions per block makes it inefficient for mobility-based applications. Lightweight security and trusted exchange in IIoT with practical consensus issues are discussed in (Bhattacharya et al. n.d.).

IoT-friendly LightBlocks uses lightweight cryptographic primitives and scalable BC consensus. Local sensor nodes (LSN) find a communication hub (CH) that sends data to gateway nodes. A low-power sign encryption method for sensor data encryption and signing is proposed at GN. In an energy-efficient Proof-of-Location (PoL), only selected verifier nodes validate blocks during consensus once the data is signed. This boosts multinational throughput and lowers mining expenses. The proposed paradigm is vulnerable to reply and man-in-the-middle attacks due to industrial IoT applications. IoMT improves healthcare via medical devices and software. This system is prone to security and privacy attacks on healthcare data. The creators of AIDSC (Garg et al. 2022) proposed an AI-based secure communication method for IoMT, intended to protect against attacks and weaknesses. The network and threat models describe IoMT device network configurations and threats. This architecture is subject to anonymity and cannot be removed when the device exits the network.

Digital signatures are cryptographic procedures that verify the validity and integrity of digital documents or messages. They give a method for verifying the sender's identity and detecting content manipulation. In the context of secure digital evidence systems, digital signatures are critical to maintaining evidence validity and integrity. Blockchain technology, which is a distributed ledger that is tamper-resistant and protects privacy, has been presented as a solution for safe digital evidence systems. It offers a decentralized and secure platform for evidence verification and management. Block-DEF, multi-signature techniques are used for evidence submission and retrieval, ensuring traceability and privacy. The use of digital signatures on the blockchain protects the integrity and authenticity of evidence, prohibiting tampering and unauthorized access. Using random and certificated key pairs in multi-signature schemes improves the security of the digital evidence architecture (Tian et al. 2019)

2.7.3 Limitations of cryptography algorithms

According to (Xu et al. 2022) this study examines the challenges that certificateless signcryption faces in an Internet of Things setting, including attacks such as Sybil, denial-of-service, tampering, key, impersonation, replay, and man-in-the-middle. It then draws attention to the necessity of establishing good traceability and regulatory mechanisms to ensure the safe transfer and sharing of data acquired by IoT devices. The significance of enabling fine-grained access control with certificateless cryptographic techniques for authentication between IoT devices and blocking illegitimate nodes from accessing these devices is also mentioned in the article.

Innovative methods for integrating BC-based solutions into Ecosystems of HIoT are discussed here. A cloud-based solution was proposed by (Anwar et al. 2017). However, this paper offers no helpful information regarding the cloud architecture's limits and potential attack scenarios. (Qu et al. 2019) reviewed the WBAN's to solve the issue of ubiquitous network availability, secure routing processes and strategies for achieving consensus are used. (Mandal et al. 2020) discussed using a certificate-free cryptographic signature in general IoT contexts to secure access control policies using a three-factor authentication system based on mobile, biometrics, and passwords. Deep learning as a service can be used to secure and sign EHRs in Healthcare 2.0 applications, as proposed by (Bhattacharya et al. 2019). Smart contracts for stakeholder interoperability, on the other hand, remain unaddressed. Using Ethereum smart contracts, (Griggs et al. 2018) presented a healthcare monitoring system that periodically examines data flow using HIoT sensors via wireless networks such as Wi-Fi and Bluetooth.

Inadequate Intelligent Sharding: Sharding, or breaking up big blockchains into smaller ones, is a technique that may be used to increase efficiency and scalability. However, a thorough analysis of intelligent sharding algorithms designed for real-time deployments in blockchain-based IoT healthcare systems is lacking in the literature. The absence of these algorithms restricts the potential for performance improvement and makes it more difficult to fully utilise the advantages of sharding.

Insufficient Performance Assessment: Frequently, prior studies have lacked thorough performance assessments that consider a broad range of communication scenarios and contrast the suggested models with current methods. It is challenging to judge the effectiveness and superiority of the suggested model over state-of-the-art methods in the absence of thorough assessments.

According to (Nguyen, Pathirana, Ding and Seneviratne 2021, Wu et al. 2021,

Rachakonda et al. 2020) suggests using blockchain-integrated privacy-assured IoMT frameworks, privacy-preserving access control, and decentralised architecture for edge-based blockchains to address these problems. These frameworks can be applied to distributed computing scenarios with low complexity and high QoS levels. However, these models have little reconfigurability or are extremely complex when used for real-time monitoring applications. Furthermore, these models' internal configuration—which isn't adaptable to newer threats—determines how secure they are. The next section of this text discusses a novel hybrid metaheuristic model for enhancing the security performance of healthcare IoT deployments in order to get around these limitations. The model's real-time usability for a multitude of use cases was validated through evaluation under a wide range of scenarios.

2.8 IoT security using optimization techniques

IoT security solutions leveraging optimization techniques harness mathematical algorithms and methodologies to fortify the security and resilience of IoT ecosystems against cyber threats. These techniques are pivotal in addressing various security challenges inherent in IoT deployments, including device vulnerabilities, data privacy concerns, and network breaches.

One key application of optimization techniques in IoT security is in the development of intrusion detection and prevention systems (IDPS). By employing machine learning algorithms and optimization methods such as genetic algorithms or particle swarm optimization, IDPS can effectively analyze IoT device behavior and network traffic patterns to detect anomalous activities indicative of potential security breaches or attacks. These techniques enable IDPS to adapt dynamically to emerging threats and minimize false alarms, thereby enhancing overall security effectiveness.

2.8.1 Role of Optimization techniques in IoT Applications

Researchers have put forth a wide range of models to optimise the security performance of IoMT deployments. For example, the work in (Zaman et al. 2022, Wang, Chen, Tie, Shojafar, Kumar and Kumari 2021) suggests integrating a multiple keyword search verification model based on pseudo-random functions and using Holochain for distributed security. For a wide range of deployments, these models help to improve both security and privacy performance. but isn't scalable for more extensive network uses.

In order to address this problem, work in (Zulkifl et al. 2022) suggests using a Blockchain-Based Adaptive Security Method that is Fuzzy. This method helps to improve security by integrating fuzzy search mechanisms that lessen deployment complexity for use cases involving large-scale networks. This architecture uses authentication, authorization, and audit logs to improve security and service quality for many application scenarios. Comparable models are covered in (Rezaeibagha et al. 2020, Zhu et al. 2021, Liu et al. 2021), where researchers suggest using Redactable Signature Schemes (RSSs), Dynamic Searchable Symmetric Encryption (DSSE), and Additive Homomorphic Encryption (AHE) to improve security performance against a variety of attack types. These models demonstrate superior Quality of Service (QoS), high attack resilience, and low latency; however, they are not adaptable to novel attack scenarios.

According to (Bi et al. 2021, Amato et al. 2019, Bao et al. 2021) proposes the use of Lightweight Fine-Grained Searchable Data Sharing (LFGSDS), which helps preempt attack patterns for a wide range of attack types, and Deep Learning-Based Privacy Preservation (DLPP), which integrates Workflow Languages and Semantics with Deep Learning (WLSDL). These models can be implemented for various healthcare-related security scenarios and are very scalable. In order to identify insider attacks in large-scale scenarios, their performance can be further enhanced by using Deep Federated Learning (DLF) (Elayan et al. 2021), Decoupled Blockchain Approach (DBA) (Aujla and Jindal 2020), Lightweight and Anonymity-Preserving User Authentication (LAUA) (Masud et al. 2021), database-specific blockchains (Liu et al. 2022), and Lightweight CNN (LCNN) (Khan et al. 2019). Although these models are very effective, they cause redundancies when the number of nodes or attacks in the network use cases increases.

2.8.2 Security models using Optimization techniques

Models that integrate blockchains for improved security performance but do not use blockchain logs for preemptive analysis include Deep Learning with Blockchains (DLB) (Rathore et al. 2021), Permissioned Blockchain with Deep Reinforcement Learning (PDRL) (Liu and Li 2022), and similar approaches. Blockchain Logging Contracts (BLC) (Chinaei et al. 2021), Blockchain-Based Secure with Lightweight Authentication (BSLA) (Yang et al. 2021), and Congestion based authentication (Ahmad et al. 2018) are some of the solutions that address these problems. They can be used in a variety of application scenarios and help to improve security and privacy performance through preemptive analysis under large-scale use cases.

Similar models are covered in (Gope et al. 2020, Li et al. 2020, Zhang, Sun, Jin, Lin and Liu 2021), wherein the use of Software Defined Network (SDN), Physical Unclonable Function (PUF), and Service Level Agreements (SLAs) is suggested as a means of enhancing the model's performance across a variety of use cases. These models combine efficiency hashing techniques with high levels of security to improve their performance in real-time attack scenarios. (Azeem et al. 2021, Meng et al. 2019, Ray et al. 2021) discuss extensions to this model that make use of SDN with firewalls, Blockchain IoT Electronic Health Record (BIoTEHR), and Lightweight Data Aggregation (LDA). BIoTEHR helps store healthcare datasets efficiently through Interplanetary

File System (IPFS) mechanisms. These mechanisms can be expanded through the use of Elliptic Curve Digital Signature Algorithm (ECDSA) (Xiong et al. 2021), Software Guards (SG) (Gao et al. 2021), Privacy Optimised Blockchains (Egala et al. 2021), and Blockchain Enabled Authenticated Key Management Protocol (BEAMP) (Garg et al. 2020), which can be applied to large-scale hospital deployments. These mechanisms are helpful when storing datasets from multiple hospitals. These models are known for their high security and low complexity, but their higher energy consumption makes them less deployable.

Improving the effectiveness of healthcare through IoMT deployment performance optimisation has been the subject of numerous research studies (Zheng, Xu, Zheng, Zhou, Yan and Zhang 2022, Yun et al. 2019, Hong et al. 2022). Several techniques have been examined in these studies, including models for QoS optimisation. However, most of these current models (Zheng, Xu, Luo, Zheng, Zheng, Chen, Zhou, Yan and Zhang 2022, Huang et al. 2022, Cai et al. 2021) have scaling issues and are not fully able to handle the unique problems that IoMT installations face. Blockchain technology has drawn attention as a potential security and efficiency solution for Internet of Things and Mobile Technologies (IoMT) deployments. Blockchain offers an immutable, decentralised ledger for keeping track of transactions and maintaining data integrity levels. However, due to their distinct features, such as mining throughput, block mining ratio, latency, and energy requirements, traditional QoS optimisation models are inappropriate for blockchain-based IoMT deployments (Huang et al. 2020, Mizrahi and Rottenstreich 2020, Kim 2019).

2.8.3 Mayfly Optimisation

To overcome these constraints, this paper suggests a novel bio-inspired model for improving the temporal QoS performance of IoMT deployments. The model makes use of the Mayfly Optimisation (MO) Method, which enables the assessment of mining performance with respect to latency, energy consumption, block mining ratio, and throughput. These performance metrics are employed to create a fitness function that establishes the appropriate split or merger of underlying blockchains based on various scenarios. Previous studies in the field of blockchain-based Internet of Things healthcare deployments have significantly helped to overcome a number of challenges. However, upon closer examination, some shortcomings and restrictions become apparent, calling for more study and creativity. The goal of this paper is to correct these errors and offer a fresh approach to improving the effectiveness and security of these deployments.

Scalability Restricted: A lot of the optimisation techniques currently in use that are suggested for blockchain-based IoT healthcare deployments complicate the mining process, which makes it harder to scale. Often, the increased complexity leads to a decrease in overall output, energy efficiency, and mining velocity. Consequently, real-time deployments are vulnerable to performance constraints that adversely affect the efficiency levels of healthcare. Other strategies that increase scalability without sacrificing security must be developed due to the limitations of these optimisation techniques.

Many optimisation models have been put forth to improve Quality of Service (QoS) in Internet of Things (IoT) healthcare deployments; however, they often ignore the temporal dimension of mining performance. Current models overlook the dynamic nature of blockchain networks and instead focus on throughput, energy consumption, and other isolating metrics. Due to this restriction, QoS optimisation is compromised, especially when it comes to latency, energy consumption, block mining ratio, and mining speed.

Inadequate Intelligent Sharding: Sharding, or breaking up big blockchains into smaller ones, is a technique that may be used to increase efficiency and scalability. However, a thorough analysis of intelligent sharding algorithms designed for real-time deployments in blockchain-based IoT healthcare systems is lacking in the literature. The absence of these algorithms restricts the potential for performance improvement and makes it more difficult to fully utilise the advantages of sharding. Insufficient Performance Assessment: Frequently, prior studies have lacked thorough performance assessments that consider a broad range of communication scenarios and contrast the suggested models with current methods. It is challenging to judge the effectiveness and superiority of the suggested model over state-of-the-art methods in the absence of thorough assessments.

It is clear that the research described in this paper is required in light of the gaps and restrictions in the body of existing literature that have been identified. In blockchain-based IoT healthcare deployments, the suggested Mayfly Optimisation Model offers a novel way to solve scalability issues, enhance temporal QoS performance, and make it easier to implement intelligent sharding algorithms. Notable advancements in block mining performance, energy consumption, throughput levels, and mining speed show how important it is for this research to close current gaps and progress the field.

The blockchain is split into two equal parts during split operations, while blockchain fragments are preserved for later retrieval during merging operations. The suggested model seeks to maximise block mining performance while accelerating mining speed, lowering energy consumption, and raising throughput levels. The effectiveness of the suggested model is demonstrated by comparison with traditional QoS optimisation models, which yields significant gains in a number of performance metrics. By addressing the shortcomings of current optimisation models and utilising bio-inspired techniques, the proposed model presents a promising way to improve the security and effectiveness of blockchain-based IoMT deployments in healthcare settings.

2.8.4 Limitations of Optimization techniques

Improving the effectiveness of healthcare through IoMT deployment performance optimisation has been the subject of numerous research studies (Zheng, Xu, Zheng, Zhou, Yan and Zhang 2022, Yun et al. 2019). Several techniques have been examined in these studies, including models for QoS optimisation. However, most of these current models (Zheng, Xu, Luo, Zheng, Zheng, Chen, Zhou, Yan and Zhang 2022, Huang et al. 2022, Cai et al. 2021) have scaling issues and are not fully able to handle the unique problems that IoMT installations face. Blockchain technology has drawn attention as a potential security and efficiency solution for Internet of Things and Mobile Technologies (IoMT) deployments. Blockchain offers an immutable, decentralised ledger for keeping track of transactions and maintaining data integrity levels. However, due to their distinct features, such as mining throughput, block mining ratio, latency, and energy requirements, traditional QoS optimisation models are inappropriate for blockchain-based IoMT deployments (Huang et al. 2020, Mizrahi and Rottenstreich 2020).

To overcome these constraints, to author (Kim 2019) suggests a novel bio-inspired model for improving the temporal QoS performance of IoMT deployments. The model makes use of the Mayfly Optimisation (MO) Method, which enables the assessment of mining performance with respect to latency, energy consumption, block mining ratio, and throughput. These performance metrics are employed to create a fitness function that establishes the appropriate split or merger of underlying blockchains based on various scenarios.

Previous studies in the field of blockchain-based Internet of Things healthcare deployments have significantly helped to overcome a number of challenges. However, upon closer examination, some shortcomings and restrictions become apparent, calling for more study and creativity. The goal of this paper is to correct these errors and offer a fresh approach to improving the effectiveness and security of these deployments (Hong et al. 2022).

Scalability Restricted: A lot of the optimisation techniques currently in use that are suggested for blockchain-based IoT healthcare deployments complicate the mining process, which makes it harder to scale. Often, the increased complexity leads to a decrease in overall output, energy efficiency, and mining velocity. Consequently, real-time deployments are vulnerable to performance constraints that adversely affect the efficiency levels of healthcare. Other strategies that increase scalability without sacrificing security must be developed due to the limitations of these optimisation techniques.

Many optimisation models have been put forth to improve Quality of Service (QoS) in Internet of Things (IoT) healthcare deployments; however, they often ignore the temporal dimension of mining performance. Current models overlook the dynamic nature of blockchain networks and instead focus on throughput, energy consumption, and other isolating metrics. Due to this restriction, QoS optimisation is compromised, especially when it comes to latency, energy consumption, block mining ratio, and mining speed.

2.9 Statistical evaluation of the Reviewed models

After a thorough examination of current IoT security models, it was found that these models differ in their operational characteristics and can be used for various real-time IoT deployments. In order to assess their performance, this section compares the models using the following metrics: P1-computational delay (D), P2-energy consumption (E), P3-security levels (Se), P4-deployment complexity (DC), and P5-scalability (Sc). The metrics were classified into low values (LV = 2), medium values (MV = 3), high values (HV = 4), and very high values (VH = 5) ranges according to their internal design and implementation characteristics. By comparing these models, researchers will be able to find the best-performing models for various application scenarios. This comparison can be observed from table 2.3. Based on this review, it can be observed that existing models require integration with Machine Learning Methods for improving their internal performance and computational efficiency for real-time use cases.

Table 2.3 Statistical evaluation of different IoT security models.

Model	P1	P2	P3	P4	P5
Blockchain-based auditable access control (Han et al. 2021)	High	Medium	Medium	High	Very high
Quantum Behaved Particle Swarm Optimization (Ghorpade et al. 2021)	Medium	Low	Medium	Medium	High
Blockchain 3.0 and Healthcare 4.0(B3H4) (Kumar et al. 2020)	Very High	Medium	High	Medium	Very high
Centreless User-Controlled Single Sign-On (Le et al. 2022)	High	High	Medium	Low	High
Physically Unclonable Functions (Zhang, Li, Liu, Hu and Zheng 2021)	Medium	Medium	High	High	Very High
GAN (Zhang, Wang, Kumar, Jiang and Shi 2021)	Very High	High	High	Very High	Very High

Continued on next page

Table 2.3 – continued from previous page

Model	P1	P2	P3	P4	P5
Distributed IP Mobility Management (Shin et al. 2019)	High	Low	Medium	Very High	High
Student Health Services (Algarni 2019)	High	High	High	High	Medium
Software-defined networking (Farris et al. 2018)	High	Medium	High	Very High	High
Blockchain Technology- Fog (Hassija et al. 2019)	Very High	Medium	Medium	Very High	Very High
AC PBS (Bera et al. 2021)	Medium	High	Medium	High	Medium
Software-defined networking ALAM (Mohanta et al. 2020)	High	High	Low	Very High	High
Software-Defined Networking (Sood et al. 2019)	Medium	Medium	Medium	Very High	High
STS (Zhang et al. 2020)	High	Medium	Medium	High	Medium
Authentication and Key Agreement (Deebak et al. 2019)	Medium	High	Low	High	Medium
SDSec (Iqbal et al. 2020)	Medium	High	High	Medium	High
OSCORE (Wang and Jin 2019)	High	Medium	Medium	High	High
BAKMP (Garg et al. 2020)	High	High	High	High	Medium
Blockchain-based Fog IoT Microservice (Whaiduzzaman et al. 2021)	Medium	High	High	Medium	High
LDUGN (Zhang et al. 2019)	High	High	Medium	High	Medium
LiTi Chain (Nguyen et al. 2019)	High	Medium	High	High	Very High
HLF attribute-based access control (Sun et al. 2021)	Very High	Medium	Medium	Medium	High
IoV Chain (Ma et al. 2020)	High	High	High	High	Very High
Space-Air-Ground- IoT (Wang, Su, Ni, Zhang and Shen 2021)	High	High	Medium	Medium	High

Continued on next page

Table 2.3 – continued from previous page

Model	P1	P2	P3	P4	P5
Block BDM (Zhaofeng et al. 2019)	High	Medium	High	Medium	Very High
Border Chain (Oktian and Lee 2020)	High	High	High	High	Very High
IoT Deep Learning (Jin et al. 2021)	Very High	High	Medium	High	Very High
DBACP IoT SG (Neshenko et al. 2019)	Very High	High	Medium	Medium	High
UAPBC IoT (Bera et al. 2020)	High	High	High	High	High
DistB Condo (Srinivas et al. 2020)	High	Medium	Low	High	High
Dual Fog IoT (Rahman et al. 2020)	Medium	Medium	Medium	Medium	High
MAMEC (Li et al. 2019)	High	High	Medium	High	High
FS-AHP TOPSIS (Shabbir et al. 2021)	Medium	High	High	High	High
Security Performance Rank (Hussain et al. 2020)	High	High	High	High	High
Attribute-Based Access Control (Iqbal and Matulevičius 2021)	High	Medium	Medium	High	Very High
SMASMD (Liu, Han and Li 2020)	Medium	High	High	High	High
Group Chain (Fernández-Caramés 2019)	Medium	Medium	High	Very High	High
HWSN (Lei et al. 2020)	High	Medium	Medium	High	High
IoT HarP SecA (Meneghello et al. 2019)	Medium	High	Medium	High	High
IoT Praetor (Samaila et al. 2020)	Low	Medium	High	High	Very High
Identified Security Attributes (Wang, Hao, Wen, Zhang, Zhang, Hu and Lu 2020)	Medium	Medium	Medium	High	Medium

Continued on next page

Table 2.3 – continued from previous page

Model	P1	P2	P3	P4	P5
Physically Unclonable Functions (Hasan et al. 2021)	Low	High	Low	Very High	High
CATP Fabric (Xu, Wang, Li, Yu, Sun, Maharjan and Zhang 2021)	High	Medium	Medium	High	High
Distributed Ledger Technology (Nguyen, Leyva-Mayorga, Lewis and Popovski 2021)	Medium	High	Medium	High	High
NETRA (Sairam et al. 2019)	Medium	High	Medium	High	High
PMSO (Hasan and Al-Turjman 2017)	High	Medium	Low	Very High	High
IoT ICS (Chen et al. 2021)	High	High	Medium	High	Medium
Transactive Energy Management (Yang and Wang 2021)	Medium	Medium	Low	Medium	High
IoT-LAN (Sathyadevan et al. 2019)	High	High	High	High	High
Analytic Hierarchy Process (Allifah and Zualkernan 2022)	Medium	Medium	High	High	High
KU-Nodes (Liao et al. 2020)	High	Medium	Medium	Medium	High
uHealth (Iwaya et al. 2020)	High	High	High	Medium	High
MQTT (Siboni et al. 2019)	Medium	High	Medium	High	Medium
SDN-IoT (Ren, Sun, Luo and Guizani 2021)	High	Medium	Medium	Very High	High
Block-SDN (Vangala et al. 2021)	High	High	High	Very High	Very High
LSROMEH (Ren, Li, Liu and Qin 2021)	High	Medium	Medium	High	High
Lagrange coded computing (LCC) (Asheralieva and Niyato 2021)	High	Medium	High	High	High
SDN-PUF (Oh et al. 2019)	Medium	Medium	High	Very High	High

2.10 Research Gaps

Several models that are used in IoT-based smart healthcare deployments are covered in this text. In order to help readers choose the best performing models for various use cases, this discussion also compares the underlying models in terms of computational delay, energy consumption, security levels, deployment complexity, and scalability metrics. In terms of these parameters, it was found that SDNs, Blockchains, Machine Learning, and PuF models perform better than others. Additionally, it was noted that QPSO (Ghorpade et al. 2021), DMM (Shin et al. 2019), and IoT Praetor (Samaila et al. 2020, Hasan et al. 2021) had the lowest deployment costs, and they had the lowest computational delays. These findings could be combined to create low-cost, high-speed smart healthcare deployments.

Additionally, it was noted that the following have the lowest energy consumption: SDN ALAM (Mohanta et al. 2020), AKA (Deebak et al. 2019), DistB Condo (Srinivas et al. 2020), PUF (Hasan et al. 2021), PMSO (Hasan and Al-Turjman 2017), and TEM (Yang and Wang 2021). The highest scalability is demonstrated by GAN (Zhang, Wang, Kumar, Jiang and Shi 2021), DMM (Shin et al. 2019), SDN (Farris et al. 2018), BCT Fog (Hassija et al. 2019), SDN ALAM (Mohanta et al. 2020), SDN (Sood et al. 2019), Group Chain (Fernández-Caramés 2019), PUF (Hasan et al. 2021), PMSO (Hasan and Al-Turjman 2017), SDN-IoT (Ren, Sun, Luo and Guizani 2021), Block SDN (Vangala et al. 2021), and SDN PUF (Oh et al. 2019). Meanwhile, the highest security performance is demonstrated by BAAC Han et al. (2021), B3H4 (Kumar et al. 2020), PUFs (Zhang, Li, Liu, Hu and Zheng 2021), GAN (Zhang, Wang, Kumar, Jiang and Shi 2021), BCT Fog (Hassija et al. 2019), LiTi Chain (Nguyen et al. 2019), IoV Chain (Ma et al. 2020), Block BDM (Zhaofeng et al. 2019), Border Chain (Oktian and Lee 2020), IoT DL (Jin et al. 2021), ABAC (Iqbal and Matulevičius 2021), IoT Praetor (Samaila et al. 2020), and Block SDN (Vangala et al. 2021).

These observations make them extremely useful for a wide range of high-security and high-scalability applications. A novel IoT Security Performance Rank (ISRM) was created by combining these metrics. It suggests that the following metrics—PUF (Hasan et al. 2021), IoT Praetor (Samaila et al. 2020), DMM (Shin et al. 2019), PMSO (Hasan and Al-Turjman 2017), BCT Fog (Hassija et al. 2019), SDN ALAM (Mohanta et al. 2020), SDN (Sood et al. 2019), Block SDN (Vangala et al. 2021), BAAC (Han et al. 2021), PUFs (Zhang, Li, Liu, Hu and Zheng 2021), ABAC (Iqbal and Matulevičius 2021), Group Chain (Fernández-Caramés 2019), SDN-IoT (Ren, Sun, Luo and Guizani 2021), SDN PUF (Oh et al. 2019), GAN (Zhang, Wang, Kumar, Jiang and Shi 2021), and DistB Condo (Srinivas et al. 2020)—have the best overall performance in terms of delay, deployment cost, energy efficiency, security, and scalability levels, making them useful for various applications. In the future, researchers can expand these models by fusing various deep learning techniques with security frameworks. This will improve the model's applicability for real-time deployments and make it secure and aware of quality of service. In addition, Q-Learning and bioinspired techniques can be combined with these models by researchers to enhance the real-time application performance in various healthcare scenarios.

2.11 Summary

This article explores IoT-based smart healthcare implementation models. This discussion analyzes models based on computational delay, energy consumption, security levels, deployment complexity, and scalability aspects to help readers choose the appropriate model for their use cases. Cryptography, blockchains, machine learning, and optimization models outperformed others in these criteria. Researchers can enhance these models by integrating deep learning approaches with security frameworks, making them more secure and QoS-aware, and making them more suitable for real-time deployments. Additionally, researchers can enhance real-time application performance by integrating Q-Learning and bioinspired approaches with these models in various healthcare contexts.

In this work, the motivation stems from the dual objective of HySSA: firstly, to establish unwavering trust among healthcare stakeholders, and secondly, to enable seamless real-time automation. In pursuit of these goals, we strategically select a local cluster head (CH) member capable of executing computationally intensive procedures. This CH collaborates with nearby sensor nodes to transmit data, which is then subjected to signcryption by local miners at the Gateway Sensor Node (GSN). After the encryption process is completed, the shared data is safely stored in the local BC client application. Taking our commitment a step further, GSN keeps a copy of this critical information within the global chain structure, replete with public identification details. To meet the needs of remote users, we use the InterPlanetary File System (IPFS) protocol to store sensor data and encryption keys securely and reliably. Ultimately, the HeaL scheme aims to reduce end-to-end latency, promoting scalability in mined transactions. Our inspiration stems from the pressing need for a holistic solution that not only ensures confidence among healthcare stakeholders but also facilitates real-time automation in the era of Healthcare 4.0.

CHAPTER 3

A Hybrid Secure Signcryption Algorithm for IoMT Security

3.1 Introduction

The IoMT connects medical devices and apps. Patients, medical professionals, researchers, and insurers benefit from the Internet of Medical Things, which enables remote medical assistance, data insights, medication management, operations augmentation, tracking patients, employees, and inventory, and more. One-third of IoT devices will be in healthcare by 2025; this proportion is expected to climb to about 40% of total global IoT technology value (i.e., $6.2 trillion). Furthermore, almost 60% of healthcare firms have already used IoT solutions, with that proportion predicted to climb to nearly 87% by the end of 2019 (Cano and Cañavate-Sanchez 2020). Security and privacy vulnerabilities are among the most critical challenges affecting IoMT solutions. The FBI has warned that existing IoMT devices are highly vulnerable to exploitation because of insufficient authentication and outdated hardware, among other reasons. The IoMT has been at the forefront of cyber attacks in recent years. According to previous polls, over 90% of IoT-enabled healthcare organizations have reported at least one security issue (Hamza et al. 2020).

The healthcare system is overwhelmed with data in today's culture. Because this data is so valuable, its security is a huge issue. Traditionally, essential patient health data is preserved in a file, and a few personal details are saved in the hospital administration database. As a result, the conditions that arise when the file is lost are somewhat tricky. A medical health card is used to get around this situation. This card provides the patient's whole medical history, including medical documents. As a result, sensitive data security is crucial. There are various encryption techniques available to ensure both data and network security (Mandal et al. 2020). It is vital to choose the finest among them. As a consequence, a lightweight elliptic curve cryptography approach is used. Compared to earlier asymmetric cryptographic algorithms, this technique provides efficient and robust data security with a reduced key size. As a consequence, no memory space is thrown away.

Health care has evolved from a hospital-centric to a patient-centric model in the last decade. Healthcare 4.0 is a paradigm shift from Healthcare 1.0. has resulted in a change in health records management from being done manually to being done decentralized and responsively. Transform Analytics predicts HIoT devices to reach 24.1 billion by 2022, growing at a CAGR of 9% annually (Hamza et al. 2020). Although sensor transmitting and receiving data occurs through readily available channels, it is vulnerable in response to network threats in the ecosystem, and there are harmful entities. As a result, mechanisms for protecting individual privacy and facilitating secure data exchange among medical stakeholders were created (Patel et al. 2020). To maintain the healthcare ecosystem's inherent responsiveness, lightweight encryption techniques were developed to facilitate data exchange via embedded sensors. Because it keeps an immutable ledger of recorded transactions, BC is a viable option for guaranteeing sequenced EHR data. Trust and chronology are important considerations (Mehta et al. 2020). Even though BC overcomes the fundamental privacy and trust issues, Mining requires a lot of energy and performance, making it resource-intensive.

To deal with issues like permitting ecosystems based on low-power calculations, frequent disconnections, and heavy offloading schemes, edge services (Bhattacharya et al. 2020) and high percentage networks (Srivastava et al. 2019) were examined by researchers. Because of that, the solutions described above are not appropriate for significant HIoT ecosystems and cannot be scaled up linearly. Therefore, researchers worked on Low-power IoT protocol stacks with extended transmission ranges, such as 6lowPAN, LoRa, and SigFox, which are used for substantial machine communications, to exploit a practical low-powered and energy-efficient consensus construction with minimum packet overheads (Liu, Liu, Liang, Chai, Lei and Zhang 2020) and minimal encapsulated headers. Encapsulation can only be as small as is necessary for security reasons (Liu, Li, Jiang, Obaidat and Vijayakumar 2020, Zeadally et al. 2021) Once a user has been authenticated, shared secret keys are used to securely exchange data.

To ensure choice recommender models in real-time can function, conventional encryption schemes aren't a viable option because of their computational complexity and resource requirements (Tanwar et al. 2019). In HIoT, PSN is used in the same way. Local coordinators are elected by the PSN in WBAN. Signcryption schemes, based on the outgoing addresses in the packet headers, have been dubbed by local-coordinators (LC). The system protects the privacy and integrity of patient information for a wide range of medical professionals (Mandal et al. 2020). With parallelism, it is possible to add security options to packets via lightweight mechanisms, improving the interest of healthcare stakeholders in responsive automation. Thus, the authors present a safe Signcryption technique that provides efficient mining operations in the study.

A Blockchain block represents the most recent data. It includes information from both the past and the future. Blocks preserve transactions permanently. Add new transactions to existing ones. Blockchain data is encrypted for security and transparency. The authorization function can be included to protect the healthcare system. Critical data is stored on the edge server for fast access. This article stresses allowing patients to access their health information from anywhere using a card reader while protecting essential data. Encrypted files are permanently saved on the blockchain. A blockchain is a decentralized digital ledger for all transactions. Blockchain transactions are separated into blocks, and cryptographic keys utilize a hash function to link them. Node-linked shared ledgers store these secret keys. The chain's duplicate data is updated and synchronized at every node.

There are various reasons for the IoMT's inadequate security, which results in such assaults Tian et al. (2019). The wide range of intrinsically vulnerable IoMT technologies, such as wireless sensor networks and cloud computing, has caused several security vulnerabilities due to complexity and incompatibility. IoT deployment in healthcare has been hurried without sufficient security consideration. A survey indicates that just 17% of device makers and 15% of medical staff are aware of IoMT security vulnerabilities and actively endeavor to prevent them (Alsubaei et al. 2019). OWASP lists typical IoMT system components. (1) Endpoints The FDA defines connected medical devices as IoT endpoints, which are connected to hospital networks, the Internet, or other medical devices. The current study examines non-medical IoMT equipment, such as ambient sensors for completeness. (2) Gateways connect weak endpoints to the backend as bridge networks. (3) Backend: IoT systems run IoMT solutions and analyze and store data via backend servers. Mobile devices and apps are used to remotely control endpoints, manage backends, and send quick notifications in IoT systems.

This chapter further organized as follows. There are a total of five sections in this article. Section II discusses the proposed HySSA scheme. Section III presents the results and analysis. Section IV presents the comparison of security features. Finally, Section V concludes the paper.

3.2 Overview of the Proposed work

This study addresses the need for a secure and efficient system for exchanging electronic health records. The utilization of different linked devices, such as wearables (like fitness trackers and smartwatches), medical equipment (like blood pressure monitors and glucose meters), and other sensors built into healthcare equipment, is referred to as the "Internet of Things". Healthcare professionals may track and keep tabs on their patients' health problems remotely, thanks to HIoT. Patients with chronic conditions, the elderly, or those needing constant monitoring may find this helpful. Existing systems may involve high costs, complex encryption processes, and limited transaction throughput. The proposed HySSA system uses blockchain technology and lightweight signcryption techniques to overcome these limitations. The problem is the lack of a cost-effective and efficient solution for securing EHR exchange through enabled device transmissions. The present methods are inefficient in computation and communication, have low throughput, and incur large transaction and signing costs. These challenges hinder the widespread adoption and secure exchange of EHR data. The proposed solution, HySSA, employs a two-stage operation. Patient wireless personal area networks (WBANs) are created using proximity sensor nodes (PSNs) in the first phase. The PSNs define the cluster head (CH) that can send EHR metadata to the WBAN's gateway sensor nodes (GSN). In the second phase, the GSN implements a lightweight signcryption technique for authorized stakeholders, combining data encryption and signing. The system utilizes the interplanetary file system (IPFS) for secure key access and exchanges data over open channels. Contributions made through this work are mentioned as follows.

1. When transmitting patient data via Internet of things, a Blockchain-envisioned strategy is presented to secure patient data trust and automation.

2. The cluster head selection process begins only after the GSN receives the patient's sensor data. This step reduces the delay in transmission.

3. Increasing the capacity of the BC network, a novel signcryption algorithm that permits low-power, energy-efficient calculations on miner nodes are offered.

3.3 The system design

The system model and the overview of the recommended approach is presented in this section. This section describes a BC - envisioned encryption technique for maintaining healthcare data confidentiality in HIoT-based ecosystems using embedded sensors and WBAN.Additional details pertaining to the system model are presented in Fig.3.1. PU stands for "patient," $N_{(CH)}$ stands for "cluster head node," $N_{(AP)}$ stands for "check point," $N_{(BC)}$ is an abbreviation for "local BC client application". $N_(M)$ stands for "miners to add transactions to BC" in our definition of the network model set in the proposed scheme as $N_U = \{N_1, N_2 \ldots, N_3,\}$ etc., are the l patients in the N_U. Each patient has k sensors $(S_1, S_2, ..., S_k)$ that are strategically placed on the N_U at predetermined locations.

It is possible for the sensors to form different WBAN regions, depending on the patient's specific monitoring requirements. Consider the case where k sensors are grouped into n regions, each of which is designated as $\{K_1, K_2, ..., K_n,\}$ and each of which has a corresponding CH, which is designated as C_n. K_n sends messages to C_n, who delivers them locally. The abundance of computing power in the immediate vicinity of C_n led to its selection. CH $N_{(AP)}$ receives data that has been aggregated by C_n. Mobile apps, fixed computers, and devices with built-in router modules can all be used as $N_{(AP)}$.

The node transmits the data. M is the manager of the kernel, and C is the module that controls it. NBC uses JSON is a JavaScript object notation talk to the local miner entity N_M, while M manages the system call stack trace. It is the NM's job to add blocks to the NBC as they are needed. A key fetch from IPFS storage is used to authorize access to $N_{(AP)}$ data by various healthcare stakeholders. $N_{(GB)}$, the public global miner, adds the generated signcrypted data N_d via S.

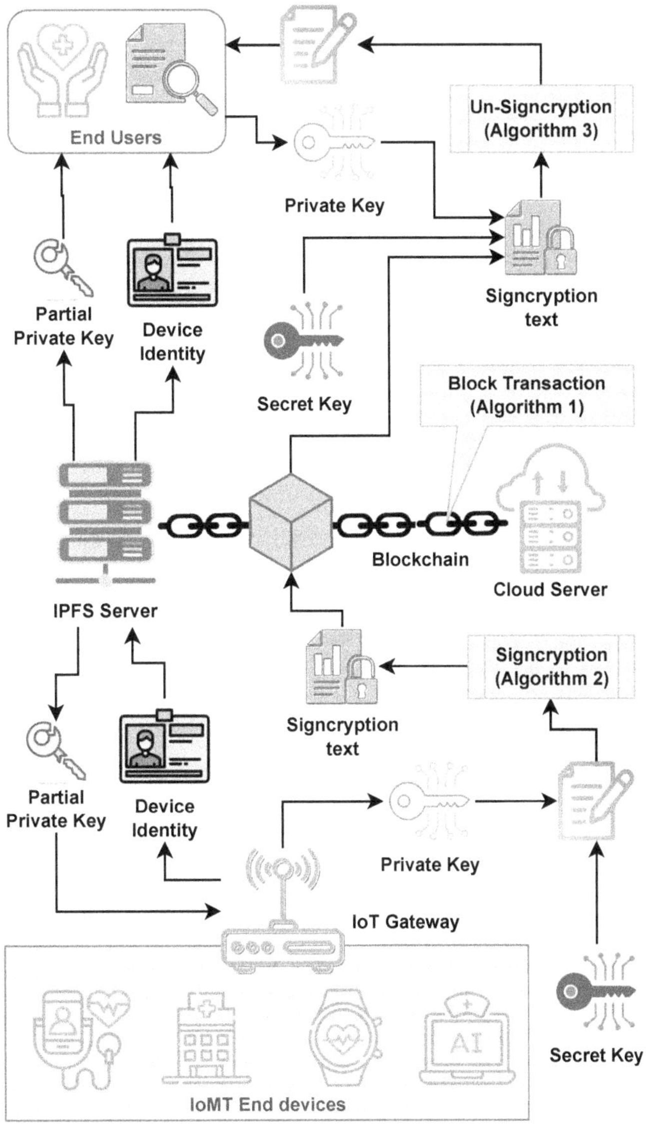

Fig. 3.1 Overview of the proposed model.

Any n^{th} cluster can choose a native C_n to send aggregated data to $N_{(AP)}$ in the proposed system model. $N_{(BC)}$ receives data in JSON format from $N_{(AP)}$'s control module C. Secure transmission of forwarded data is made possible with our proposed signature scheme S, which is sent to $-NM$ for addition at the local $N_{(BC)}$. Now that the specifics of the HySSA plan have been revealed.

3.4 IoMT Network deployment and Patient Registration phase

In any given K^{th} cluster, there may be as many as l patients, denoted by the letters $\{N_1, N_2, ..., N_l.\}$ As depicted by the $M : U_l \rightarrow S.$ mapping, these l users typically use k sensors. Because it correlates numerous sensor units with any U_l, the mapping M is many-to-one. During the registration phase, the patient must authorize a local BC client application node. In order to send data to $N_{(BC)}$, U_l must upload the EHR data saved in the client application.

$$K_{Ul} = \{ID_{Ul}, M, ID(C_n), EHR^{Ul}, GSN - id\} \tag{3.1}$$

Which includes the identity of $ID_{(Ul)}$, the identity of CH C_n, $EHR^{(Ul)}$, and the identity of the forwarding GSN in addition to that of the uploaded EHR data. In the example below, the wallet attributes for U_l are generated based on $K_{(Ul)}$.

$$W_{Ul} = \{ID_U, (PVT_l, PBC_l), CU_l, T, M_{(root)}\} \tag{3.2}$$

The two main private public key pairs are Markel root (M_{root}) and $(PVT_t - PBC_t)$, (CU_t) represents the crypto-currency unit for exchanging the data in wallet. It's now possible to collect data from a sensors dentoed as $S_a = \{S_1, S_2, S_3, ..., S_a\}$ at regular intervals, such as the user's pulse rate or blood pressure. As a result of this mapping, U_l is now referred to as $M : U_l S_a$. Aggregated and sent through C_n to the gateway sensor node GSN, which is labelled with the GSN_{id}, the mapped data. the PVC_l, PBC_l are used to forward the mapped data D_{Sk}, which is defined as $M_2 : U_l DS_l$ in the mapping definition shown below.

$$M_2 = \{D_{S1}, D_{S2}......., D_{Sk}\} \tag{3.3}$$

Control module C_n collects data for transmission to the network point $P_{(AP)}$ based on $D_{(SK)}$ and sends it to the control module C. There is a a restriction on the number of transactions that can be performed added to a given block of ledger BL in the latter method. According to this BL data Kumari et al. (2020).

$$BL = \{BL_{ID}, HS_{pv}, GSN_{id}, VR_{bl}\} \tag{3.4}$$

This information includes the verifier's block hash, the local block identifier $(BL_{(ID)})$, as well as the hash of the previous block. An indexed key $IN_{(ks)}$ is created based on the BL between In order to mine the local block state information, transactions and block ids must be used. These Are All the key Parameters of $IN_{(Ks)}$.

$$IN_{ks} = \{BL, HS_{cr}, DS_{sk}, l\} \tag{3.5}$$

where l is the current timestamp is represented An index pair entry list is created based on the associated parameter information, and subsequent rows are denoted as $IN = \{IN_{n1}, IN_{n2}, ..., IN_{nl}\}$. Approved transaction lists are stored in CUR_{bl} by VR_{bl} using hashes $H(t)$ appended to the list. GSN creates a lightweight signcryption scheme S for IN once the index structure has been verified, abbreviated as GSN_t. If a block validation chain list was successful or unsuccessful, then a $BOOLEAN$ variable w will be set to indicate this fact. Algorithm 1 explains the preceding concept. There are n cluster regions in which algorithm 1 operates, and l patients are embedded with k sensor units in each of these clusters. As a result, algorithm 1 has a time complexity of $O(ntq)$. We need a linear space chain because we store linked block state information in an indexed list structure. Space has an $O(n(l+k))$ level of complexity.

Table 3.1 List of key notations

Notation	Description
ID_{ul}	Identity information
ID_{Cn}	Identity of cluster node
CUt	Crypto-currency unit
T^U	Timestamp
M_{root}	Merkle root
$(PV_k - PB_k)$	Private-public key pairs
BL_{ID}	Local block identity
HS_{pv}	Hash of the previous block
VR_{bl}	Verifier blocks
l	current timestamp
$Delta_n$	Partial private key
$MSKY$	Master key
T_a	Trusted Authority
SP_j	Service providers
SM_i	Smart meter
RA	Registration authority
RID_{RA}	Pseudo-identity of the RA
TID_{SMi}	Temporary identity of Smart Meter
TC_{SPj}, TC_{SMi}	Temporary credentials of SPj and SMi, respectively
$Cert_{SPj}$, $Cert_{SMi}$	Certificates issued by the RA to SPj and SMi, respectively

3.5 Blockchain Creation and Transaction phase

Initialization and registration of patients: Block validation information is produced during this phase utilizing previously collected and current hash information from blocks that have already passed through the procedure. The $HS(T.pv)$ and $H(T.cr)$ is Hexadecimal hashes for the accurate updating of the blocks, $HS(T.pv)$ should be included

Algorithm 1 Verification of block transaction according to Index-wise.

Input: Set of TRS Transaction
Output: w = {0,1}; a Boolean variable indicating the success or failure of block-verified transactions, VR_{bl}.

Procedure (TRS) Verification
$IN_{ks} \leftarrow \{BL, HS_{cr}, DS_k, l\}$
$H_{cr} \leftarrow Hash - Append\left(HS_{pv}, IN_{ks},\right)$
if $(HS(T:pv) \in HS(T:cr))$ **then**
$VR_{bl} \leftarrow Append\left(TRS, BL\right),$
Call $SIGNCRYPTIONS.$
$w \leftarrow 1$
output "**list validation block validation SUCCESS**"
else
$VR_{bl} \leftarrow Reject\left(TRS, BL\right),$
$BROADCAST(B)$
$w \leftarrow 0$
output "**list validation block validation FAILED**"
end if
end Procedure

in $H(T.cr)$. Upon meeting the criterion, a signcryption scheme S is offered. T_a is considered a trusted authority variable in our $WBAN$ system's GSN layer. Using the Control module and kernel call stack status M, GSN overlay is responsible for forwarding signed and verified patient data.

As a result of the GSN overlay $GTW - n$ forming an overall $WBAN$ structure for the validated data, it sends a request to T_a to begin the signcryption process. $Prv(Key)$ Z_u is a private key that is produced at random. $Pub(Key) = prv(Key)$, which is how Z_u calculates the $publickey(Key)$. $Prv(Key)$ can only be seen by Trusted Authority but IP. The complete procedure is shown in Fig.3.2. Following is an explanation of how the GTW_n and C_n registration phases work in the same way:

1. The trustworthy authority, T_a, GWT_n receives the identifying information. For identifying the public and private key pairs by using retrieved public information from the T_a information.

2. Sensors are assigned by the Cluster Head to collect data DT_n inside the cell's range. CHs are cluster leaders receive a private key, $Prv(Pk)$, from trusted authority T_a in exchange for safe processing; as a result, $Pub(P_k) = prv(P_k)$ yields the public key (P_k).

3. T_a Finally, the $n^{(th)}$ cluster calculates the secret value that provides salt to the transaction.

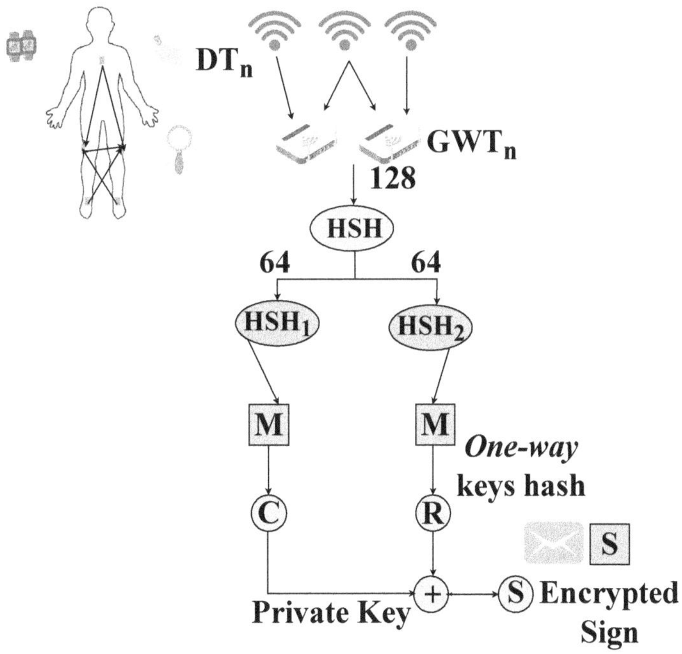

Fig. 3.2 Proposed signcryption architecture.

We compute the following to register the user U_l's phase.:

1. U_l selects an anonymous key, $SCR_U \epsilon Z^*_\alpha$ as well as computes public information.
2. U_l securely submits $\{ID_U; Q_U\}$ to T_a on Q_U.

   T_a generates the partial private key Δ_n shown below.

$$\Delta_n = \{HSH(Q_n) \parallel ID_n \parallel ID_{cn}\} \tag{3.6}$$

3. Using Δ_n , U_l determines the Number of private key as pk_n = Δ_n:Q_n, multiplies by it $Z^*_{\|}$.
4. The entire private key pk_n = $\Delta_n.Q_n$ as ECC-point multiplication in $Z^*_{\|}$, for user U_l . To create a patient signature, the patient's biometric β_n is Collected and a secure password is generated τ_n.

Public parameters fixed in cluster sensor nodes allow T_a to access the data held by cluster heads C_n are the created parameters (Sn). On the basis of a safe password, the secret-key information k is derived.

$$\eta_k \leftarrow (k^*_u, T_A) \tag{3.7}$$

The overlay gateway GSN_T has been secured with the master key $MSKY$

$$MSKY \leftarrow SHA - 256(\tau_n \parallel L_u \parallel ID(VR)_{bl} \|)\eta_n) \tag{3.8}$$

When two nodes are compared using $MSKY$, the communication point is found to be on the curve $Eq(m, n)$ and signatures can be generated for both the gateway nodes and the patient nodes. Similarly, two temporary points A_1 and A_2 and random integers $\{v_1, v_2, v_3\}$ on E_q were selected (m, n). Then, GSN and U_n receive A_1 and A_2, respectively. These values (a_1, b_1, a_2, b_2) were arrived at using the information provided in the following way:

$$(a_1, b_1) = v_1.G + k_U.N_G(a_2, b_2) = v_2.G + k_U.Y_{S_m} \tag{3.9}$$

For SP_1 and SP_2 and one-way hash functions HSH^1 and HSH^2, partial signatures like (c_1, d_1) are computed, as well as one-way keyed hash functions. In order to compute gateway and patient node signatures SP_1 and SP_2, two secret functions γ_1 and γ_2 based on combined encryption, designated as R, are calculated.

Signatures of the king and queen The gateway's and the patient's $Sign_G$ and $Sign_U$ are computed on the final R. Finally, the signer's details are confirmed and recorded in Block B of the local chain. The algorithms for signing and verifying have now been fully defined.

3.6 Signcryption Algorithm phase

The subject matter of this discussion Verified transactions are used to generate the patient and gateway node hash keys. In order to continue signing transactions, you'll need these keys. As a result, the terms "private/public sender/receiver pairs," or $\{PV_S, PUB_S\}$, have been coined. Pair values are then used to build parameters for secure data routing in clusters C_n. Protecting the network's nodes and boundaries from external and internal threats is the purpose of this phase Elhoseny and Shankar (2019). In-depth information on the upcoming the phase of signcryption is now accessible.

1. When a WBAN control device, such as a mobile phone, is used, a random number is generated from the range of 1 through $(q - 1)$, where q refers to the integer set Z. Assume X is the number to be utilized..

2. It's time to build a 128-bit hash of PUB_S, which is the public key of the control unit, and the integer X.

$$Hsh = Hash(PVT_R mod PN) \tag{3.10}$$

3. HSH is further subdivided into two 64-bit sections, HSH_{s1} and HSH_{s2}.

4. c is the cipher text created by the key HSH_{s1} for the message relating to patient

health alerts.

$$C = E(HSH_{s1}(M)) \tag{3.11}$$

Encryption module (E), message (M) in this case.

5. Integrating M generates a one-way keyed hash function for the $WBAN$ control center, which now utilizes HSH_{s2}. In this case, it's known as $r1$.

$$r1 = KH(HSH_M) \tag{3.12}$$

6. The $WBAN$ control center's private key is used to encrypt c and r, and a new variable, s, is created.

$$s = X/(r1 + PV_S)modPN \tag{3.13}$$

In the second algorithm, the details of the stages suggested are now provided. Algorithm 2 incorporates the signcryption procedure into its calculations.

Algorithm 2 Algorithm for Signcryption Proposal

Input: X integer, chosen at random from the range 1 to $(q-1)$ from Z, q, sender and receiver secret identifiers PV_s, PV_r, and public keys PUB_s, PUB_r, PN, KH a function that uses a one-way key the p Boolean variable, as well as the E encryption and decryption algorithms
Output: c: cypher text, r: message hash, s: message signature

procedure SIGNCRYPTION $(X_q, PV_S, PV_R, PUB_R, PUB_S)$
X $\in \{1, ..., (q-1)\}$
Compute $Hsh \leftarrow Hash\,(PV_r, modPN,)$
Compute $(Hsh_{s1}, Hsh_{s2}) \leftarrow Hsh$
Compute $c \leftarrow E(Hsh_{s1}(M))$
Compute $r1 \leftarrow KH(Hsh_{(message)})$
$s \leftarrow \frac{X}{(r1+PV_s)(modPN)}$
Return $c, s, r1$
end Procedure

As a result, algorithm 2 has a time complexity of $O(q.C_k)$ the difficulty of storing messages for q patients' bit-string vectors.

3.7 Un-Signcryption Algorithm phase

The receiver side generates a 128-bit hash of the obtained $c, s, r1$ values from algorithm 2 using the received values. For ease of computation, let's use F, which stands for a random integer of order PN selected from

$\{1, 2, ...(PN1)\}$. It's now possible to see exactly how hashing works.

$$Hsh_r = Hash((PV_R * f) * PUB_S mod PN) \quad (3.14)$$

There, Hsh_R is the computer hash at the other end. The tuple set $\{PUB_S, PV_R, P_N, f\}$ is now the focus of our calculations. The un-signcryption scheme is shown in Fig.3.3. As a result, we partition the 128-bit Hshr into two 64-bit pieces at the receiver, Hsh_{r1} and Hsh_{r2}, respectively. The cypher text c is decrypted by Hsh_{r1}, and the message M is extracted by Hsh_{r1}.

$$M = D(Hsh_{r1}(C)) \quad (3.15)$$

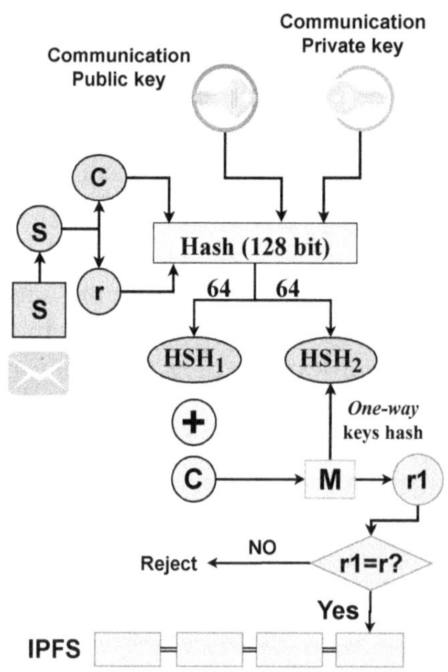

Fig. 3.3 Proposed un-signcryption scheme.

M is now hashed using Hsh_{r2} on the remote server and compared to $r1$ using a one-way keyed hash function. The message is not corrupted or tampered with if both $r1$ and $r2$ match; otherwise, the message is corrupted. This is exactly what is happening, as illustrated below.

$$r2 = KH(Hsh_{r2}(M)) \quad (3.16)$$

In C_n regions both Algorithm 2 and algorithm 3 are tested for one patient by un-signcryption process. Consequently, algorithm 3's time complexity is $O.(l.C_n)$. Message verification is required as with bit-string vectors because of the high space complexity $O(l.b_l)$.

Algorithm 3 Proposed algorithm for un-signing encryption

Input: Cipher-text c, message M hash $r1$, decryption algorithm D, and generated signature s

Output: A **BOOLEAN** indicator $p \in$ **TRUE**, **FALSE** indicated verification of the signature, either successful or unsuccessful.

procedure SIGNCRYPTION$(X, c, s, r1,)$
F $\in [1, ..., (PN-1)]$
Compute $Hsh_r \leftarrow Hash\{(PV_r \times f)\times, modPN,\}$
Split $\{Hsh_{r1}, Hsh_{r2}\} \leftarrow Hsh_r$
Compute $M \leftarrow D(Hsh_{r1}(C))$
Use a single key to compute a function $r2 \leftarrow KH(Hsh_{r2}(M))$
if $(r1 == r2)$ **then**
output "SUCCESS Signature verification"
$p \leftarrow True$
else
output FAILURE Signature verification "
$p \leftarrow False$
Return p
if end
end Procedure

3.8 Securing IoMT with HySSA in Real-time

The proposed HySSA plays an important role in securing the Internet of Medical Things (IoMT) data, safeguarding sensitive health information, and ensuring its confidentiality, integrity, and authenticity. In the proposed work, confidentiality is achieved by transforming plain text data into ciphertext through an encryption key and algorithm, ensuring that only authorized parties can access the information. With respect to integrity, the proposed encryption algorithms (Algorithm 2) often include mechanisms like hashing and digital signatures to verify that data hasn't been altered during transmission or storage. This becomes particularly important in IoMT applications where healthcare providers need to confirm that the data from a medical device hasn't been tampered with before processing or displaying it. Authentication complements encryption by confirming the identity of users and devices, reducing the risk of data manipulation by malicious actors. In a real-world scenario, a wearable medical device could use encryption keys unique to each user, ensuring that data is associated with the correct patient which is ensured in Algorithm 3.

Secure transmission is vital since IoMT devices typically communicate over the internet, which can be insecure. Encryption algorithms create secure communication channels, protecting data as it travels between devices, cloud storage, and healthcare systems. This level of security is achieved in the proposed model via less communication overhead for applications like remote patient monitoring, where continuous transmission of patient data to healthcare providers is required. Key management is also effectively managed with blockchain construction. In an IoMT setup, key management involves securely distributing keys to medical devices and healthcare systems to ensure only authorized parties can access the data. By integrating encryption algorithms in Algorithm 1 and implementing robust key management practices, IoMT systems can protect sensitive medical information, comply with regulations such as HIPAA in the U.S., and maintain the safety and privacy of patients.

3.9 Results and Analysis

This section discusses the performance evaluation of the proposed model based on parameters such as mining delay, signing and verifying costs, and system transactional throughput T. EM's observed mining delay compared to that of other cutting-edge techniques is used in the calculation. Using an Ubuntu Linux v18.04 LTS virtual computer with 8 GB of internal RAM and a 100 GB external hard drive, we are testing the secret consortium library open source (open CCF). Nod e.js v8.9.2 and npm v6.7.1 are both installed. Costs for signing and validating documents, mining performance, and storage are evaluated and the analysis were presented in the table 3.6 and table 3.5.

Table 3.2 Comparison of Security features

Features	**SCBAS-SF**	**BSKMP**	**DBACP**	**AIDSC**	**LightBlocks**	**HySSA (Proposed)**
Anonymity	Yes	No	Yes	No	Yes	Yes
Un-Traceability	No	Yes	Yes	Yes	No	Yes
Revoke Access	Yes	Yes	No	No	Yes	Yes
Mutual Authenticity	Yes	Yes	No	Yes	Yes	Yes
Integrity	No	No	Yes	Yes	No	Yes
Insider Attack	Yes	Yes	No	Yes	Yes	Yes
Replay Attack	Yes	No	No	NA	No	Yes
Man-in-Mid Attack	Yes	Yes	No	Yes	No	Yes
DoS Attack	Yes	Yes	Yes	Yes	Yes	Yes
Brute Force Attack	Yes	Yes	Yes	Yes	Yes	Yes

3.9.1 Evaluation of the HySSA's Functionality

We assume that Algorithm 2 is given The patient and gateway nodes' hash keys in order to evaluate the HySSA scheme's performance. The performance analysis has been presented with the comparison of traditional model which does not use any security algorithm for data security. The results show the performance against the signing cost, computational delay and network throughput. The Fig.3.4 depicts the transaction and signature cost delays for mined blocks. When the number of blocks mined are less, the HySSA scheme takes the communication costs as 48.56 ms and Computation costs as 104.1612. This initial performance has been improved when the number of blocks are increased. This results into Lower communication costs than the computation cost. For calculation of the signing costs each block is fixed with the size of 128 bytes and being exchanged to the control module C to the gateway GSNn results in cheap sign-and-verify fees.

Mining latency of processed blocks is shown in Fig.3.5 in comparison to the mining latency of conventional ways. The system has a mining delay of 29 ms, compared to the traditional scheme's 28.4 ms for the 50 blocks to be mined. But the HySSA proved it performance when the number of blocks are increased. This results into 4.7 ms less delay when the number of block are 500. When transactional metadata is sent across the local chain, more transactions are added to the same block, lowering latency. Mining latency, on the other hand, increases as more blocks are added until it approaches the baseline.

As shown in Fig.3.6, the scheme's network storage requirements has be evaluated and presented based on the network throughput are compared to those of a typical network. Transactional performance is increased by 20% while using HySSA to store patient data. Having only meta-information stored in a chain structure has led to an increase in transaction throughput.

Table 3.3 Computation Time analysis for various operations

Notation	**Description (Time to Compute)**	**Computation time ($\approx$ in ms)**
T_h	Hash function	0.309
T_{exp}	Modular exponentiation	0.039
T_{mtp}	Modular multiplication	0.385
T_{ecm}	ECC point multiplication	2.288
T_{eca}	ECC point addition	0.016
T_{enc}	Symmetric key encryption	0.018
T_{dec}	Symmetric key decryption	0.014
T_{sig}	Signature generation	4.495
T_{poly}	Polynomial evaluation	0.132

3.9.2 Examining the Risk

We now assess the security computation approach that takes security identifier costs into account (Srinivas et al. 2018). As a result, the computational and communication cost of the proposed model has been presented here. The computation and computational cost

Table 3.4 Message description for cost analysis

Description	Size(in bits)
Message digest(hash value)	240
Elliptic curve point	640
Random or pseudo identity	240
Timestamp	32
Random nonce	240
AES plaintext/ciphertext block	128
Message length	160

Table 3.5 Computation cost analysis

Scheme	Total Cost of Computing ($\approx$)	Time(ms)
SCBAS-SF	$9T_h$+$4T_{ecm}$	11.933
BSKMP	$12T_h$+$4T_{ecm}$ + $2T_{eca}$+$2T_{poly}$	13.156
DBACP	$11T_h$+$4T_{ecm}$ + T_{epa}	12.567
AIDSC	$16T_h$+$2T_{enc}$+$2T_{dec}$	5.012
LightBlocks	$9T_h$+$2T_{ecm}$+ $4T_{eca}$	7.121
HySSA (Ours)	$8T_h$+T_{ecm}+$2T_{eca}$+$2T_{enc}$+$2T_{dec}$	4.856

analysis has been compared against the different simulation parameters on the proposed model.

1) Computation Cost: In order to verify the transaction, HySSA first evaluates the computation costs, as indicated in algorithm 1. In addition to the two hash appends, the approach also uses a symmetric encryption key. It takes 2 (0.018+0.14) seconds to complete. Algorithm 1 requires the computation of addition and multiplication in ECC points, as well as eight hashes. This means that 8(0.309) + 2 (2.288) + 2 (0.018+0.14) seconds are needed. Unsigncryption verification algorithm 3 is presented as follows: eight hash Hsh1, one signature verification and two block add operations are presented. The time required is 8(0.309) + 2 (2.288) + 2 (0.018+0.14) + 2 (0.016) milliseconds. As a result, the proposed scheme's total computing time is 4.856 milliseconds.

Communication Cost: It's a 1 bit BOOLEAN output after the last hash block of 240 bits and a 240 bit identification for CCM. To put it another way, the total number of bits

Table 3.6 Communication costs analysis

Scheme	No.of messages	Communication cost (in bits)
SCBAS-SF	3	2272
BSKMP	3	1724
DBACP	3	3040
AIDSC	3	1792
LightBlocks	3	2530
HySSA (Ours)	3	2130

involved is 481 bits. It then requires 160 bits, three random 32-bit nonces, one 640-bit ECC operation, and a 32-bit sequence number for the identity ID. As a result, there are 608 bits total: 480 + 8 * 32 + 640 + 32 = 1408. As a result, we have one signature verification of 1 bit and a 240-bit hash identity. This means that the total number of bits required to transmit data is 240 plus one, or 241. Consequently, HySSA's total data transmission costs are 481 bits, 1008 bits, and 241 bits, which amounts to 2130 bits.

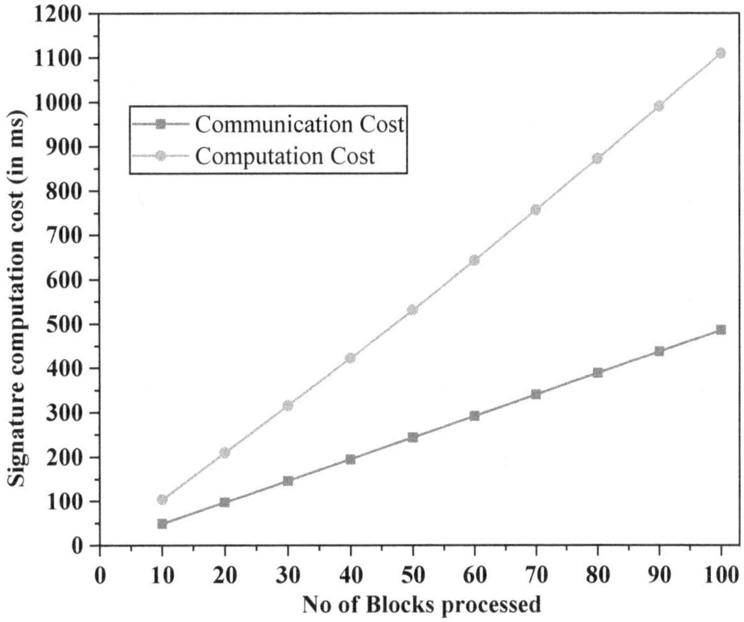

Fig. 3.4 Comparison of Signature computation cost.

3.10 Comparison of Security Features

The proposed model's security features were evaluated, and the results were compared to other relevant schemes, such as SCBAS-SF (Vangala et al. 2021), BSKMP (Das et al. 2021), DBACP (Bera et al. 2020), AIDSC (Garg et al. 2022) and LightBlocks (Bhattacharya et al. n.d.) During the login and authentication step, computation and communication costs are calculated based on the security and functionality aspects. This evaluation sheds light on the proposed scheme's efficacy in contrast to the other plans listed in Table 3.2. Table 3.3 discusses the notations used for different cryptographic techniques for comparison and computational cost estimation. We also assume that the entity's true identity, random nonce, and timestamp are each 240 bits long, 240 bits long, and 32 bits long, respectively. For symmetric key encryption and decryption, the Advanced Encryption Standard (AES-128) was used.Table 3.4 summarizes all entities and bit sizes.

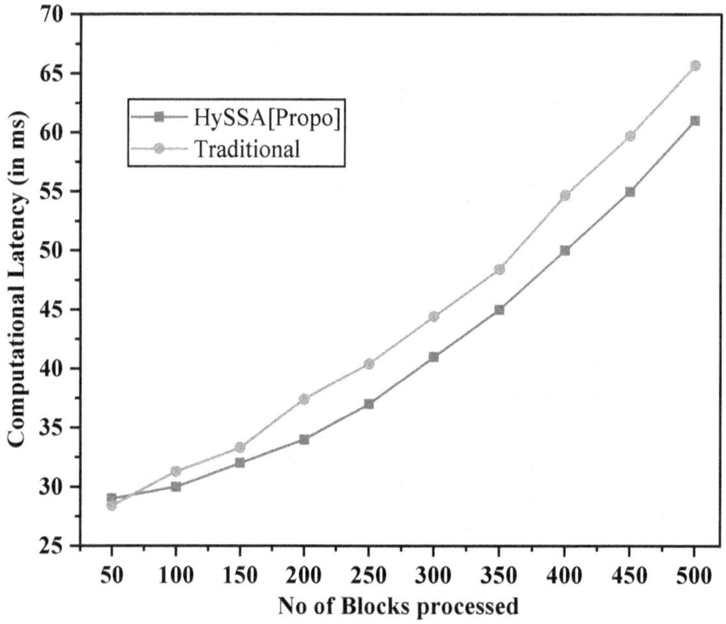

Fig. 3.5 Computational latency of the proposed model.

In Table 3.2, We compared the proposed schemes' security and functionality features to those of other schemes. It is worth noticing that SCBAS-SF (Vangala et al. 2021) is quit good compared to the proposed model except un traceability and integrity of the data communication. Also the work BSKMP (Das et al. 2021) is not good at the anonymity, integrity and prone to reply attacks. The work DBACP (Bera et al. 2020) is not good at provoking access and prone to mutual authenticity. In AIDSC (Garg et al. 2022) the security features replay attack is not evaluated and it is not applicable. Also this model is prone to Anonymity and access controls. The LightBlocks (Bhattacharya et al. n.d.) model struggles with man in the middle and replay attacks. Finally, the suggested contains a number of functional properties and is resistant to well-known assaults.

3.10.1 Security Analysis

Proposition 1: DBACP-IoTSG is secure against smart meter and SP impersonation attacks

Proof: In this proposition, it's stated that an adversary (A) cannot impersonate a smart meter (SM_i) or a service provider (SP_j) due to the secret credentials and computational infeasibility. We can break down this security property into mathematical expressions:

Smart Meter Impersonation Attack: To impersonate SM_i, A would need to compute $R1, X1$, and $X2$. The values of $R1, X1$, and $X2$ are calculated using secret cre-

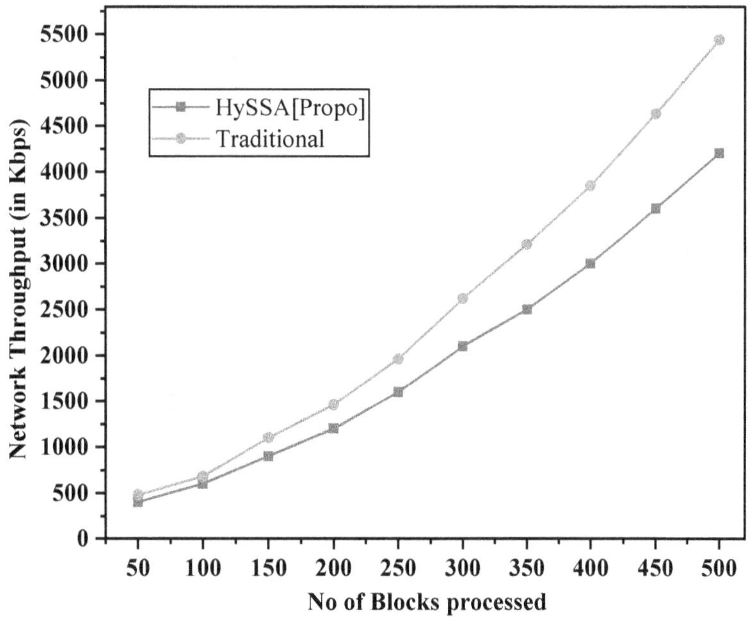

Fig. 3.6 Network throughput of the proposed model.

dentials RID_{SMi} and TC_{SMi}. A's attempt to impersonate SM_i can be expressed as follows: A's Attempt:

$$R1 = h(r1 * RID_{SMi}).G \tag{3.17}$$

$$X1 = h(TC_{SMi} * TS1) \oplus h(RID_{RA} * RID_{SMi} * TS_1) \tag{3.18}$$

$$X2 = h(TID_{SMi} * RID_{SMi} * RID_{RA} * R1 * Cert_{SM}i * TS_1) \tag{3.19}$$

Without knowledge of RID_{SMi} and TC_{SMi}, A cannot compute $R1, X1, andX2$ as they are based on these secret credentials. Thus, SM_i impersonation is computationally infeasible for A.

Service Provider Impersonation Attack: To impersonate SPj, A would need to compute R2, $DKji$, Y1, $SKji$, Y2, and $(TID * SMi)$. The values of these parameters are based on secret credentials TC_{SPj}, RID_{SPj}, RID_{SMi}, TC_{SMi}, and the session key SK_{ji}. A's attempt to impersonate SPj can be expressed as follows:

$$R2 = h(r2 * RID_{SPj}).G \tag{3.20}$$

$$DK_{ji} = h(r2 * RID_{SPj}).R1 \tag{3.21}$$

$$A\ calculates\ Y1 = h(TC_{SPj} * TS2) \oplus h(RID_{RA} * RID_{SMi} * TS1 * TS2) \tag{3.22}$$

A attempts to compute $SKji$ and $(TID * SMi)$

Proposition 2:DBACP-IoTSG is resilient against smart meter physical capture attack

Proof: This proposition states that even if a smart meter (SMi) is physically captured, the compromise of its unique credentials does not affect the security of other non-compromised smart meters. Let's express this property mathematically: The set of unique credentials (uc) for each smart meter can be represented as follows:

$$SMi's_{(uc)} = \{TID_{SMi}, RID_{SMi}, TC_{SMi}, Cert_{SMi}\} \tag{3.23}$$

$SMi's$ Credentials = $TID_{SMi}, RID_{SMi}, TC_{SMi}, Cert_{SMi}$ The compromise of $SMi's$ credentials does not impact the security of other smart meters, represented as: Compromise of $SMi's$ Credentials $\neq$ Compromise of Other Smart Meters' Credentials This mathematical expression signifies that compromising the credentials of one smart meter does not enable an attacker to compromise the credentials of other smart meters in the network.

Proposition 3:Replay attack is protected in DBACP-IoTSG

Proof: This proposition states that replay attacks are protected by including timestamps and random numbers in messages. Mathematically, we can express this as follows: Messages sent in the access control phase include timestamps and random numbers:

$$Msg1 = \{TID_{SMi}, X1, R1, X2, Cert_{SMi}, TS1\} \tag{3.24}$$

$$Msg2 = \{TID * SMi, R2, Y1, Y2, Cert_{SPj}, TS2\} \tag{3.25}$$

Verification of timestamps ensures message integrity and freshness: If Timestamps in Received Messages $\neq$ Timestamps in Original Messages Then, the message is considered invalid and rejected as a replayed message. This mathematical expression demonstrates that the algorithm's use of timestamps helps detect and prevent replayed messages.

Proposition 4:The man-in-the-middle attack is protected in DBACP-IoTSG

Proof: This proposition states that the algorithm is designed to withstand man-in-the-middle (MITM) attacks. We can express this mathematically as follows: In an MITM attack, the adversary may intercept a message $Msg1$ from an insecure channel and attempt to generate a valid message Msg1' to the receiver SPj. The ability to generate a valid Msg1' requires knowledge of preloaded secret credentials:

$$DKji = h(r2 * RID_{SPj}).R1 \tag{3.26}$$

$$R1 = h(r1 * RID_{SMi}).G \tag{3.27}$$

Without knowledge of these secret credentials, the adversary cannot produce valid messages, thus preventing the MITM attack:
A's Attempt: $Msg1 \neq Msg1'$ This mathematical expression confirms that the algorithm's use of secret credentials prevents adversaries from successfully carrying out MITM attacks. These mathematical expressions provide a formal representation of the security properties outlined in the propositions. However, it's essential to conduct a thorough cryptographic analysis and formal proof to ensure the algorithm's security rigorously.

Proposition 5:DBACP-IoTSG is resilient against the ESL (Eavesdropping, Session Disclosure, and Long-Term Key Disclosure) attack

Proof: This proposition asserts that the algorithm ensures the confidentiality of session keys and preserves perfect forward secrecy. We can represent this mathematically as follows: The session key shared between a smart meter (SMi) and a service provider (SPj) is calculated as:

$$SKij = h(DKij * h(TC_{SMi} * TS1) * h(TC_{SPj} * TS2) * Cert_{SMi} * Cert_{SPj}) \tag{3.28}$$

The session key is the combination of session-temporary (ephemeral) credentials (random numbers) and long-term secrets (secret credentials and pseudo identities). Even if an adversary compromises a session key $(SKij)$ for a specific session, it does not enable them to calculate session keys for other sessions. This is due to the use of distinct short-term and long-term secrets for each session:

$SKij \neq SKji$ for Different Sessions

This mathematical expression demonstrates that the algorithm's design prevents the disclosure of session keys across different sessions, ensuring the confidentiality of sessions and preserving perfect forward secrecy.

Data Confidentiality is a critical aspect of data security that involves protecting personal or sensitive information from unauthorized access and disclosure which is assessed as,

$$Pr[Adv(C, E(K, M)) = 1] \leq \varepsilon \tag{3.29}$$

Where: Adv$(C, E(K, M))$ represents the advantage of an attacker (Adv) distinguishing between ciphertexts (C) of two different messages (M) encrypted with the same key (K). ε represents a negligible probability. Let $E(K, M)$ denote the encryption of a message M with a cryptographic key K. For a given message M and key K, the encryption $E(K, M)$ using the hybrid secure signcryption algorithm provides a level of security where the probability of an attacker successfully recovering the original message M is negligibly small.

Data Integrity H(M) remains unchanged during transmission and storage, and for any message alteration,

$$Pr\left[H\left(M'\right) \;=\; H\left(M\right)\right] \;\leq\; \delta \tag{3.30}$$

Where: $H(M)$ denotes the hash of a message M. M' represents the altered message. δ represents a negligible probability. Let $H(M)$ denote the hash of a message M. The hybrid secure signcryption algorithm ensures data integrity by guaranteeing that for any message M, the hash $H(M)$ remains unchanged during transmission and storage, and any alteration to the message can be detected with high probability.

Entity Authentication can be achieved through various methods, categorized broadly into something the user knows, something the user has, and something the user is, often referred to as the factors of authentication. This work assessed as,

$$Adv\left(EA\left(\Pi\right)\right) \;\leq\; \varepsilon \tag{3.31}$$

Where: EA(Π) represents an entity authentication experiment for protocol Π. Adv(EA(Π)) represents the advantage of an attacker in successfully impersonating an entity in protocol Π. ε represents a negligible probability. Let P and Q represent two entities (e.g., a smart meter and a medical server). The algorithm guarantees entity authentication, ensuring that P can prove its identity to Q, and Q can verify P's identity, with a negligible probability of impersonation or man-in-the-middle attacks.

Key Management Security Effective key management is crucial for maintaining the confidentiality, integrity, and availability of sensitive data. The proposed work manages the key sharing as

$$Pr\left[Adv\left(KM\right) \;=\; 1\right] \;\leq\; \varepsilon \tag{3.32}$$

Where: $Adv(KM)$ represents the advantage of an attacker (Adv) in compromising key management mechanisms. ε represents a negligible probability. Let K1 and K2 represent cryptographic keys used in the algorithm. The key management mechanism of the hybrid secure signcryption algorithm provides secure key generation, distribution, and storage, making it computationally infeasible for an attacker to deduce K1 or K2 from available information.

Resistance to Cryptographic Attacks Let A be an attacker and Adv be the advantage of A in breaking the algorithm. The hybrid secure signcryption algorithm resists known cryptographic attacks, such as chosen plaintext attacks, chosen ciphertext attacks, and brute-force attacks, ensuring that $Adv(A)$ is negligibly small.

Compliance with Regulatory Standards The hybrid secure signcryption algorithm complies with regulatory standards (e.g., HIPAA, GDPR) related to data security and privacy in healthcare, and its design and implementation adhere to the specified requirements.

Usability and User Acceptance User studies and usability assessments confirm that healthcare professionals can effectively and efficiently use the algorithm without significant usability issues or disruptions to their workflow.

Testing and Evaluation Rigorous testing, including formal security testing and evaluation against known vulnerabilities and attack scenarios, demonstrates that the hybrid secure signcryption algorithm meets its specified security objectives and withstands potential threats.

Documentation and Compliance with Security Standards The documentation associated with the hybrid secure signcryption algorithm includes comprehensive mathematical specifications, security proofs, and cryptographic standards compliance, ensuring transparency and ease of audit. These propositions provide a starting point for a mathematical evaluation of the algorithm's security properties. However, they should be further refined, formalized, and subjected to rigorous cryptographic analysis and proofs to ensure the algorithm's security in a real IoMT environment.

3.10.2 Comparison Analysis

The proposed HySSA scheme has a low consumption of 20000 J for n = 500 block additions, compared to 23000 J in SCBAS-SF, 21000 J in BSKMP, 21900 J in DBACP, 24000 J in AIDSC and 22200 J in LightBlocks respectively. Each model only includes transactions that have been validated through the transaction pool and meet the consensus window boundary criterion. Thus, only new transactions of blocks are sent through cluster heads, that results in improved energy consumption of the proposed model showing Fig.3.7.

The result of Fig.3.8 displays the mining latency of the suggested model in comparison to other similar examined approaches, as determined by the encryption model's block adds. The suggested method has a mining delay of 29 ms for 50 block adds, compared to AIDSC's 27 ms. The mining latency for 500 block adds is 61 ms, compared to 65 in AIDSC, 62 in SCBAS-SF, 68 in BSKMP, and 67 in Light Blocks methods. Signcryption keeps track of the sorted key structure of each block and checks that the block hashes H(T) at the same time to make sure they match addresses from blocks before. This means that every second, more transactions are added to the same block, which

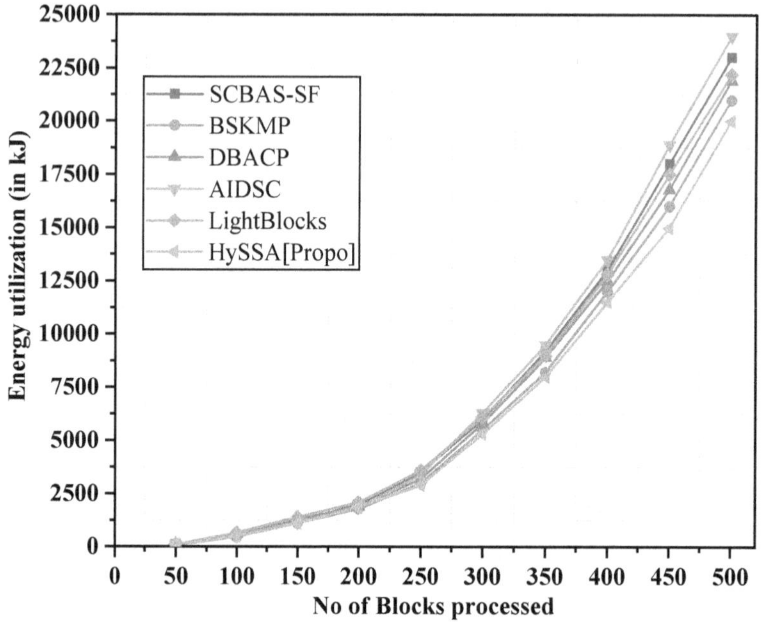

Fig. 3.7 Comparison on Energy utilization.

makes mining processes more efficient.

In this section, we compare the measured techniques to the obtained transaction throughput in terms of their efficiency. The same is presented in Fig.3.9. The proposed system clearly has utilization of 400:4200 kbps at 50:500 appended transactions to the transaction pool. While the baseline system does not use lightweight consensus, the suggested approach does so that it can maximize resource utilization within the confines of a window. The rate is determined after the transactions are added to the transaction pool. In addition, we can adjust system utilization by changing the frequency f at which blocks are added to the chain, or alternatively, by increasing the amount of data passed through the N IoT nodes, which permits greater burst loads to pass and keeps transaction throughput constant.

The Fig.3.10 shows the trust probability as shown in LightBlocks (Bhattacharya et al. n.d.). In a public chain, there is the potential for more than 50% of miners in the network to collude by introducing more hash power from the same community, lowering trust and invalidating the newly added block, allowing malicious entities to grow the side-chain The network will accept the chain with the longest growth rate, so a private chain using the PoL consensus mechanism will keep intruders out of our network.

According to Fig.3.11 compared the node commit latency to the industry standard methods. Since the block can be processed by the consensus method more quickly than on any other public chain network, the block can be committed more quickly. As evaluated, the proposed model produce less node commit delay as 485 ms when 100

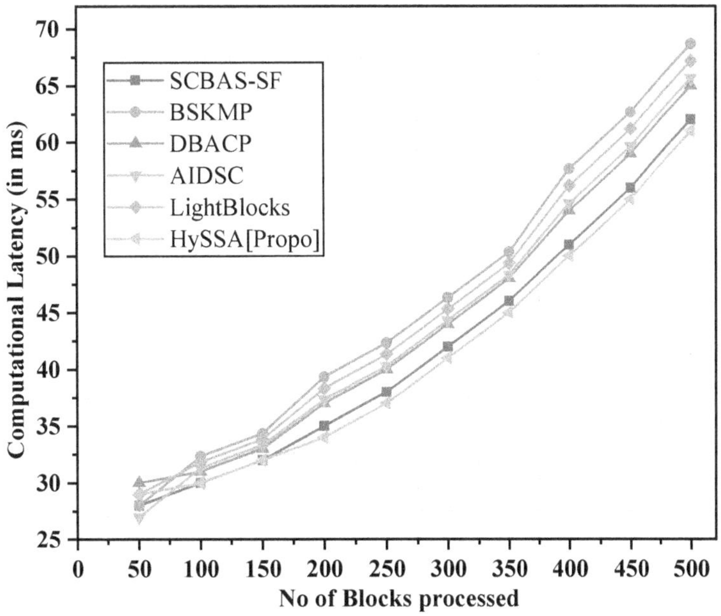

Fig. 3.8 Comparison on computational latency.

blocks are processed at each node. This results has been taken from the average of computation run from 10 blocks to 100 blocks on each node. The same scenario has been evaluated against other related model and it produces the delay of 1193 ms in SCBAS-SF, 1315 ms in BSKMP, 1256 ms in DBACP, 501 ms in AIDSC and 712 ms in LightBlocks.

In the Fig.3.12 presents the signing delay against the baseline approach LightBlocks (Bhattacharya et al. n.d.). As the graph shows, the signature latency climbs in proportion to the amount of transactions in a block, so the suggested model has an advantage over the baseline techniques with a delay of 1110 milliseconds for a block containing 100 transactions. In the existing model LightBlocks (Bhattacharya et al. n.d.), the communication delay has been achieved as 1965 ms which produces 855 ms more delay.

3.10.3 Computation Cost Analysis

The showing Table 3.3 based on existing experimental results, how long does it take to execute various cryptographic primitives SCBAS-SF (Vangala et al. 2021), BSKMP (Das et al. 2021), DBACP (Bera et al. 2020), AIDSC (Garg et al. 2022), LightBlocks (Bhattacharya et al. n.d.). The login and authentication phase also undergoes a cost-of-computing comparison study in Table 3.5. The SCBAS-SF measures represent an estimated increase in computational costs associated with the suggested method in comparison to existing approaches (Vangala et al. 2021). Using the existing experimental results given in Table 3.6. 11.933 ms, BSKMP (Das et al. 2021) : 13.156 ms, DBACP (Bera et al. 2020) : 12.567 ms, AIDSC (Garg et al. 2022) : 5.012 ms, LightBlocks

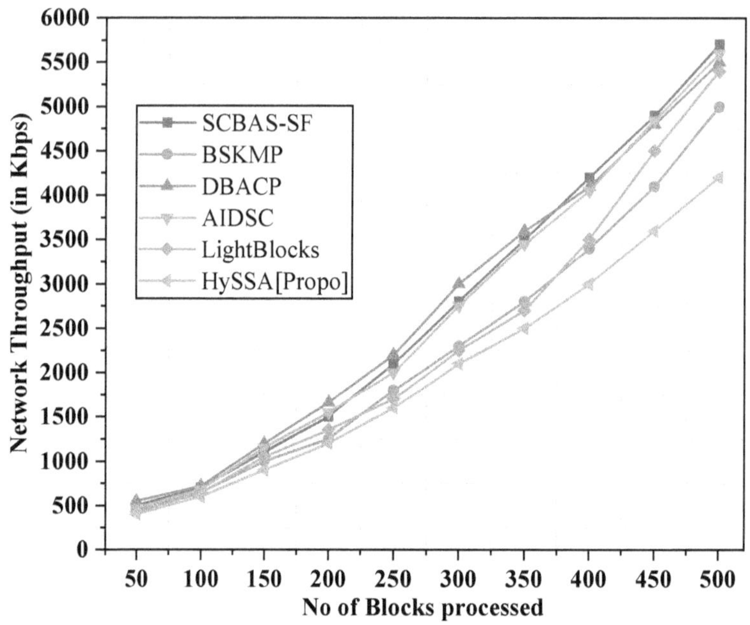

Fig. 3.9 Comparison on Network throughput.

(Bhattacharya et al. n.d.) : 7.121 ms and the proposed model achieves less computation cost 4.856 ms.

Thus, resource-constrained wearable sensor nodes benefit from the suggested scheme. Table 3.5 shows that the proposed system has a lower computation cost than all other schemes except LightBlocks (Bhattacharya et al. n.d.). Despite higher computing costs than LightBlocks (Bhattacharya et al. n.d.), the suggested approach offers superior functionality and security to Table 3.2.

3.10.4 Communication Cost Analysis

To assist in a comparison of communication costs, the following assumption has been made: The bit lengths required for an identity, a random nonce, a timestamp, a certificate with an elliptic curve digital signature (LightBlocks (Bhattacharya et al. n.d.)), hash output (if we apply SHA-1 as AIDSC (Garg et al. 2022)), and message authentication code (MAC) are, respectively, 320, 320, 480, 480, 320, and 320 bits. In addition, there are 1024 bits. To ensure proper security, modulus is employed for modular exponentiation and inversion operations in this comparative analysis.

A comparison study on communication overhead comparison during the login and authentication phases is completed in Table 3.6. Device pairing-based authentication (also known as DPA) and challenge-response-based authentication are the two types of authentication that may be used with the LightBlocks system (CRA). LightBlocks' DPA and CRA protocols impose a communication cost of 2530 bits each bit sent or received

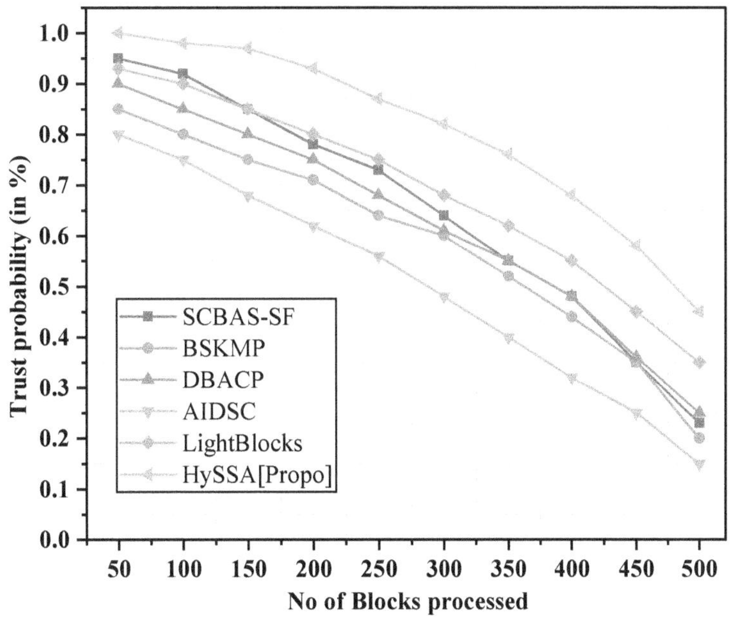

Fig. 3.10 Comparison on Trust Probability.

(for 3 messages). The communication costs that are incurred for three messages in a SCBAS-SF scheme are 1724 bits, while the communication costs that are incurred in a BSKMP system are 3040 bits.

According to the plan that has been suggested, the people who are speaking with one another are required to send and receive a total of three messages. It is necessary to have 1024 bits for Message1, 320 bits for Message2, and 480 bits for Message3 accordingly. As a result, the total cost of communication for the exchange of three messages is as follows: become 2130 bits in length. The proposed strategy has a communication cost that is comparable to that of other models' strategies. When compared to BSKMP and AIDSC, the suggested method delivers greater security along with expanded functionality. As a result, the higher communication costs that are associated with the method are comprehensible given these benefits see Table 3.2.

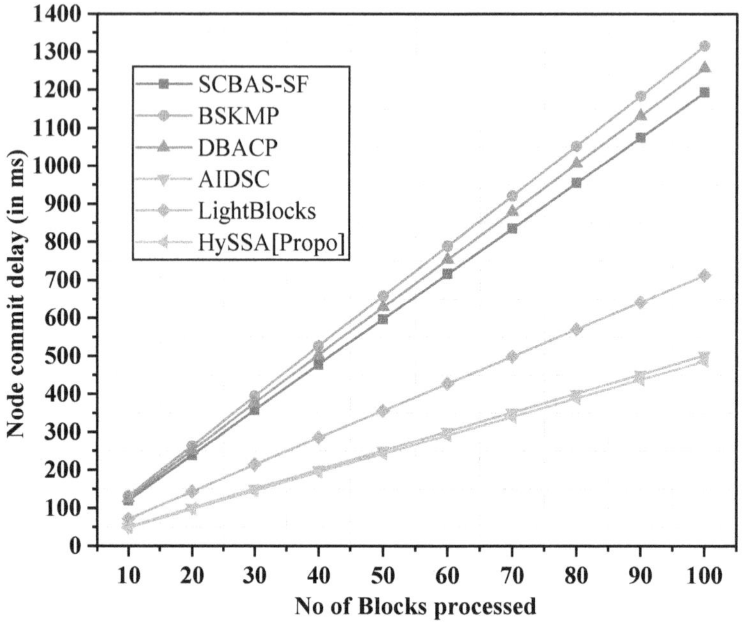

Fig. 3.11 Comparison on node commit delay.

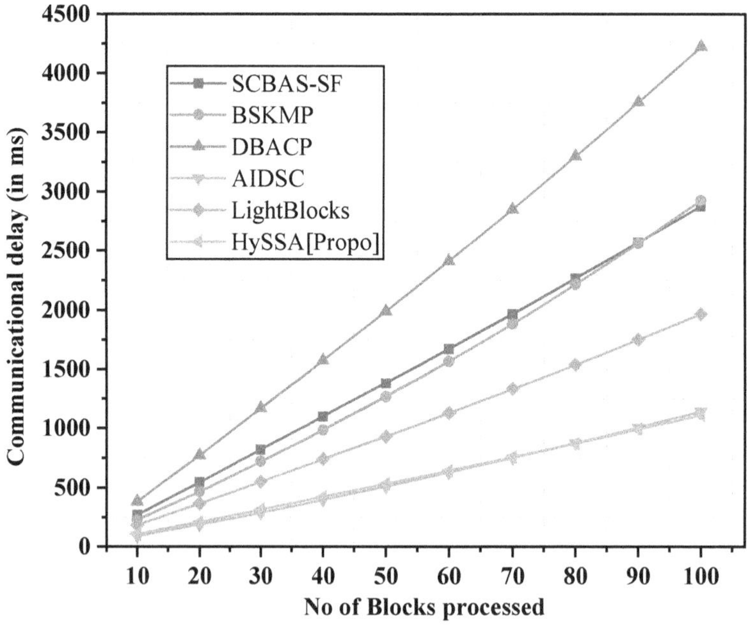

Fig. 3.12 Comparison on communication delay.

3.11 Summary

This research proposes HySSA, a blockchain-enhanced strategy for decentralised healthcare IoT ecosystems. The proposed protocol for healthcare IoT data exchange is characterised by its rapidity, responsiveness, and resilience. Additionally, nodes designate a local cluster head to distribute meta-electronic health record data to gateway sensor nodes. IPFS-obtained signature encryption keys are utilised by registered healthcare stakeholders on edge devices. Metadata is validated by local miners before being appended to the BC ledger. After confirming the transaction state, local BCs propagate the transactions to the global chain. The results obtained from the analysis indicate that the suggested approach is more feasible in comparison to the other options.

Simulation results demonstrate the effectiveness of the HySSA system. It achieves a faster signing time of 3.32 seconds and a verification time of 6.52 seconds compared to traditional schemes. Mining 200 blocks takes 3.325 seconds, outperforming the traditional schemes' time of 7.8 seconds. The transaction throughput of HySSA reaches 142.78 Mbps, surpassing the standard 102.45 Mbps. Additionally, the proposed approach showcases a competitive computing time (CC) of 45.80 ms and communication time (CCM) of 97 bytes, indicating its security capabilities. The HySSA system offers a cost-effective solution with improved transaction speeds, higher throughput, and reduced computational and communication expenses. By solving existing system limitations, HySSA can improve the security and efficiency of EHR exchange, resulting in better healthcare outcomes and patient care. The study's findings can inform the creation of future systems and contribute to advances in the field.

Subsequently, we shall examine the challenges associated with integrating the consensus on energy efficiency into the existing system. To address this concern, a consensus method that is energy-efficient, utilises fewer computing parameters, and implements the required level of security will be presented. Future work aims to enhance healthcare data security in IoMT network design using a dynamically reconfigurable hybrid metaheuristic model, utilising elephant herding optimisation and grey wolf optimisation for improved deployment security and QoS performance.

CHAPTER 4

Improving Security Performance of using Hybrid Metaheuristic Model

4.1 Introduction

Network design for the Internet of Medical Things (IoMT) is a subset of IoT that combines various medical devices to enhance real-time care operations and patient monitoring. These networks are made up of an extensive collection of gadgets that can speak with the cloud and one another to make crucial decisions about patient care. Because the security of these networks and devices is crucial, researchers have implemented a number of high-security frameworks that include features like attribute-based access control, hashing, encryption, and privacy preservation. However, the security models that are currently in use are either extremely complex or have limited reconfigurability when used with real-time monitoring applications. Furthermore, the internal configuration of current models determines their security performance and is typically not adaptable to newer forms of attack. This text discusses a novel hybrid metaheuristic model for enhancing the security performance of healthcare IoT deployments in order to get around these restrictions. Initially, the model uses a blockchain-based approach that can be dynamically changed by altering its internal hashing and encryption standards.

The underlying blockchain-based IoMT deployment's security and quality of service performance are then continuously optimised by the suggested model by combining Elephant Herding Optimisation (EHO) and Grey Wolf Optimisation (GWO). The dual fitness functions defined by the proposed model are intended to improve security and quality of service performance against various types of attacks. These fitness functions are assessed in various attack scenarios, which helps adjust hashing and encryption settings and improves overall performance in various attack scenarios. The hybrid EHGWO Model is highly scalable and practical for real-time scenarios because it can adjust the underlying blockchain-based deployment for dynamic attack scenarios. The model's performance was assessed in relation to multiple state-of-the-art models and under attacks such as distributed denial of service (DDoS), man-in-the-middle, masquerading, and Sybil. This comparison showed that the suggested model demonstrated

10.3% better network consistency under attack scenarios, 5.9% better throughput, 6.5% higher packet delivery ratio, and 8.3% faster attack detection and mitigation performance. The suggested model could be implemented for real-time healthcare use cases as a result of this performance.

Integration of multidomain modules capable of network traffic analysis, traffic representation, encryption, hashing, privacy preservation, authentication, access control, attack identification, and post-processing operations is necessary for designing a secure IoMT model. Blockchain-based security models perform better for IoMT deployments than other models, according to an analysis of several security models. This is because blockchain can be used for tamper-proof applications because it offers finer access control, better transparency, higher traceability, and immutability. Fig.4.1 illustrates a typical blockchain model Ren, Li, Liu and Qin (2021) that is used for IoMT scenarios. Smart contracts are created by combining various clinical repositories. Deep Neural Network (DNN) classifiers are used to process these contracts, helping with permission-based data access operations.

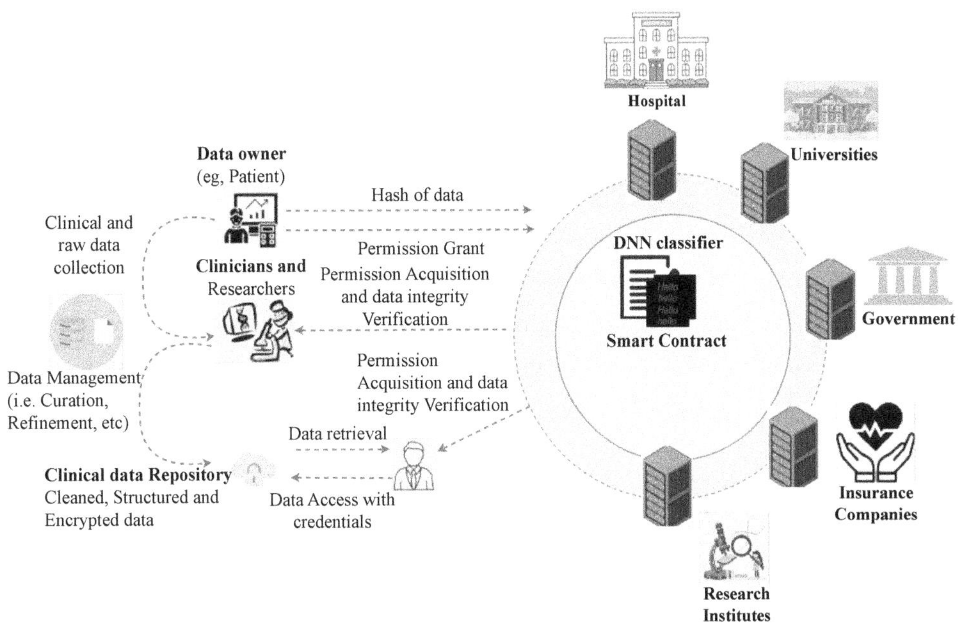

Fig. 4.1 Blockchain based IoMT Access control Model.

Interplanetary File Systems (IPFS) and smart contracts enable the model to store patient- and hospital-specific data in an unchangeable format, and DNN continuously reconfigures the blockchain to protect against various attack scenarios. In the next section of this text, similar models with varying blockchain types and optimization techniques are covered (Xu, Zhou, Tao, Liu, Yu and Kumar 2021, Besher et al. 2020, Alladi et al. 2020). This talk looks at a variety of context-specific subtleties, functional benefits, deployment-specific constraints, and future possibilities for these models that are specific to networks. Following this conversation, it was found that when it comes to real-time monitoring applications, the security models that are currently on the market are either extremely complex or not very reconfigurable. Furthermore, the internal configuration of existing models determines their security performance and is frequently not adaptable to newer forms of attacks. This is a result of the fact that current models were created to fend off common threats. Section 3 of this work presents a novel hybrid metaheuristic model for improving healthcare IoT deployment security. The model initially uses a blockchain-based method, which can be dynamically reconfigurable by modifying its hashing and internal encryption specifications.

The model integrates the Elephant Herding Optimization (EHO) and Grey Wolf Optimization (GWO) models to continuously improve security. Dual fitness functions are specified by the model under presentation, each of which aims to raise security and QoS performance against a range of attack types. Next, a range of attack configurations are used to test these fitness functions. This assessment aids in resetting the hashing and encryption parameters, which eventually improves overall performance when exposed to various attack types. Because it can adjust the underlying blockchain-based deployment for changing attack scenarios, the hybrid EHGWO Model is highly scalable and applicable to real-time scenarios. One of its primary selling points is this. In section 3.4, the model's performance was evaluated and compared with models that are thought to be at the cutting edge in terms of throughput, packet delivery ratio, network consistency metrics, and attack detection and mitigation latency under different types of attacks. Finally, some insightful observations regarding the proposed model and recommendations for future improvements to its performance round out this chapter for different operations.

4.2 Metaheuristic model

A metaheuristic algorithm is a higher-level strategy or heuristic designed to find, generate, or select a heuristic (partial search algorithm) that may provide a sufficiently good solution to an optimization problem, especially with incomplete or imperfect information or limited computation capacity. Metaheuristics sample a set of solutions which is too large to be completely sampled. Metaheuristics may make few assumptions about the optimization problem being solved, and so they may be usable for a variety of problems. In essence, metaheuristic algorithms are general-purpose optimization algorithms that can be applied to a wide range of optimization problems. They are not problem-specific but rather problem-independent, making them versatile tools for solving complex optimization problems where traditional exact methods might be impractical due to their computational complexity.

These algorithms often draw inspiration from natural processes or social behavior to guide the search for optimal solutions. They typically involve iterative improvement techniques that explore the search space efficiently, even in the presence of constraints or uncertainties. It's important to note that while metaheuristic algorithms can provide good solutions to optimization problems, they may not guarantee finding the optimal solution due to their stochastic nature. Therefore, they are particularly useful for complex problems where finding the exact solution is computationally infeasible or where near-optimal solutions are acceptable.

Grey Wolf Optimization (GWO) is a metaheuristic algorithm drawing inspiration from the social hierarchy and hunting behavior of grey wolves. It functions by simulating the leadership dynamics within a wolf pack, where alpha, beta, delta, and omega wolves represent distinct hierarchical positions. Initially, a population of candidate solutions, symbolized as wolves, is randomly generated within the problem's search space. Through iterative evaluation of fitness based on the problem's objective function, wolves adjust their positions akin to the hunting strategy of their real-life counterparts. The alpha wolf, possessing the highest fitness, leads the pack and influences the positions of the beta and delta wolves, representing the subsequent hierarchical ranks. Omega wolves, the least dominant, adjust their positions relative to the alpha, beta, and delta wolves, ensuring comprehensive exploration of the search space. GWO balances exploration and exploitation by dynamically adjusting the exploration rate throughout iterations. In the realm of security, GWO finds application in various optimization tasks such as feature selection for intrusion detection systems, parameter optimization in cryptographic algorithms, and network intrusion detection. Its ability to efficiently navigate complex solution spaces makes it a valuable tool for enhancing security mechanisms and mitigating vulnerabilities. However, customization and adaptation of the algorithm are crucial to align its functionalities with the specific requirements and constraints of security-related optimization problems.

Elephant Herding Optimization (EHO) is a metaheuristic algorithm inspired by the cooperative behavior observed in elephant herds. In this algorithm, the population of potential solutions is represented as a group of elephants navigating through a problem's search space. Each elephant corresponds to a candidate solution, and the algorithm progresses iteratively, mimicking the social interactions and decision-making processes observed among real-life elephant herds. Throughout iterations, elephants adjust their positions based on both individual fitness evaluations and collective knowledge shared within the herd. This collective intelligence allows the herd to effectively explore the solution space, balancing between exploration and exploitation to find optimal or near-optimal solutions. EHO has found applications in various optimization domains, benefiting from its ability to leverage cooperative behaviors for efficient problem-solving. However, like other metaheuristic algorithms, EHO may require customization and parameter tuning to adapt to specific problem characteristics and achieve desirable outcomes.

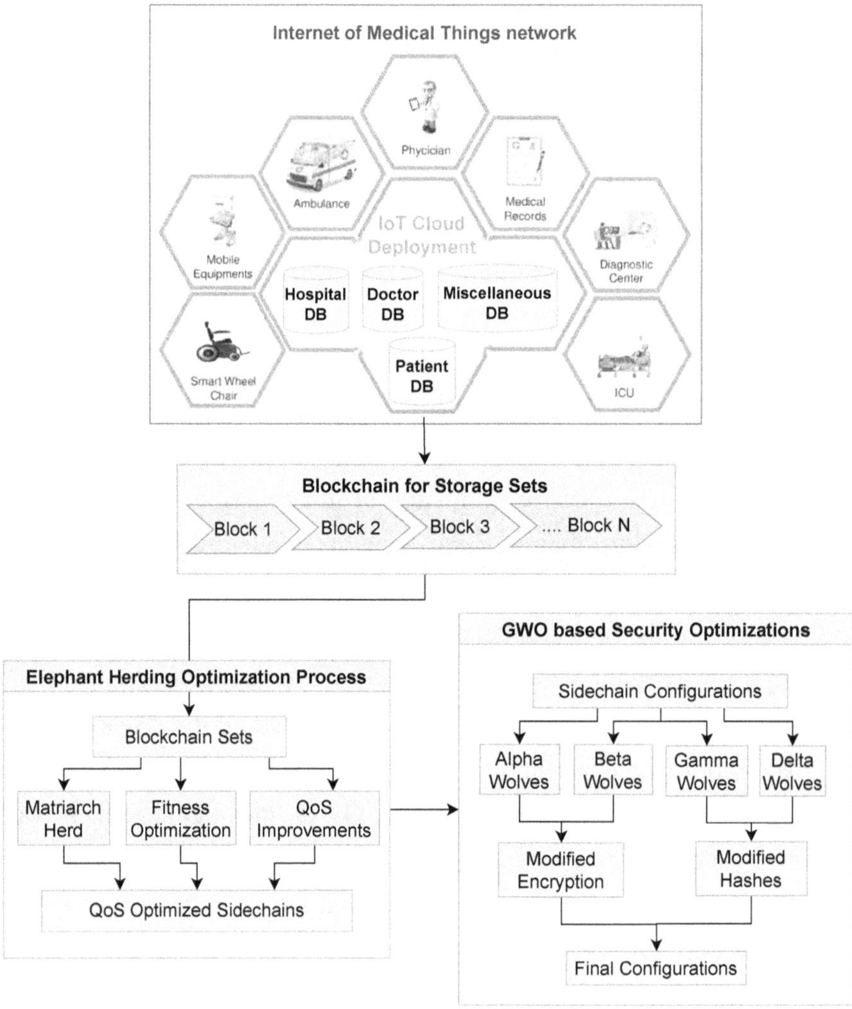

Fig. 4.2 Overview of the hybrid bioinspired security model.

4.3 Enhancing Security with Metaheuristic model

Following an examination of the security models now in use for Internet of Things-based healthcare systems, it was found that these models are either very complex or not very reconfigurable when used for real-time monitoring applications. The fact that these models are currently in use led to this discovery. Furthermore, the internal configuration of existing models determines their security performance and is usually not adaptable to newer attacks. This is so because the models in use today were created to fend off more antiquated threats. To overcome the aforementioned limitations, this section addresses the design of a novel Hybrid Metaheuristic Model for enhancing the Security performance of Healthcare IoT deployments.

Algorithm 4 HMMSHI: Joint Optimization Algorithm

Require: setup GWO and EHO constants
Ensure: Selection of miners and their configurations

Begin
for (Each configuration) **do**
    $x \leftarrow$ fitness of $max_{(D)}$
    $y \leftarrow$ fitness of $max_{(E)}$
    $z \leftarrow$ fitness of $max_{(THR)}$
    Modify solution sets as per thresholds
    Update solution sets
end for
Find security and QoS performance levels
for (each security configuration) **do**
    $i \leftarrow$ QoS levels of $max_{(D)}$
    $j \leftarrow$ QoS levels of $max_{(E)}$
    $k \leftarrow$ QoS levels of $max_{(THR)}$
    Regenerate other high QoS solutions
    Update other solution sets
end for
Evaluate security levels
for (each solution sets) **do**
    estimated high QoS
    find high configuration solution set
    apply and evaluate efficiency levels
    Continuously update the security performance
    Continuously update the QoS performance
end for
End

The model's flow is shown in Fig.4.2, where it is first implemented using a blockchain-based technique that can be dynamically reconfigured by changing its internal hashing and encryption standards. This is evident in the way the method was initially implemented in the model. The proposed model combines the Elephant Herding Optimisation (EHO) and Grey Wolf Optimisation (GWO) models to continuously optimise the security and quality of service performance of the deployed Internet of Things that is based on blockchain technology. The proposed model defines dual fitness functions, each trying to enhance the quality of service performance and security against various types of attacks. A range of attack configurations are then employed to assess these fitness functions. This assessment aids in resetting the hashing and encryption parameters, which eventually improves overall performance when exposed to various attack types. The hybrid EHGWO Model is highly scalable and practical for real-time scenarios because it can adjust the underlying blockchain-based deployment for dynamic attack scenarios.

The model initially deploys a Distributed Proof of Stake (DPoS) based blockchain, which uses a block structure as depicted in Fig.4.3.

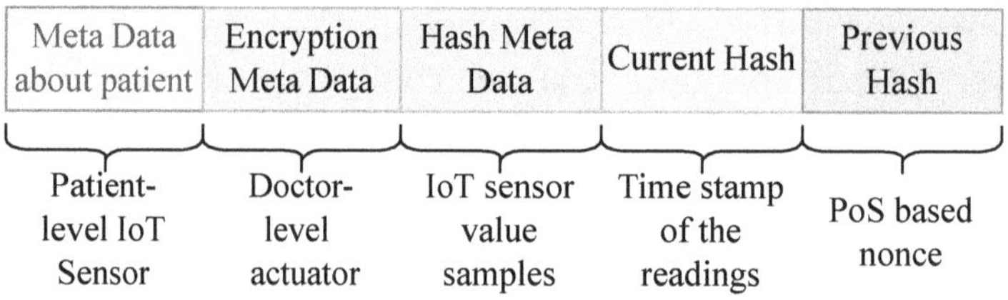

Fig. 4.3 The block structure used for deployment in IoMT.

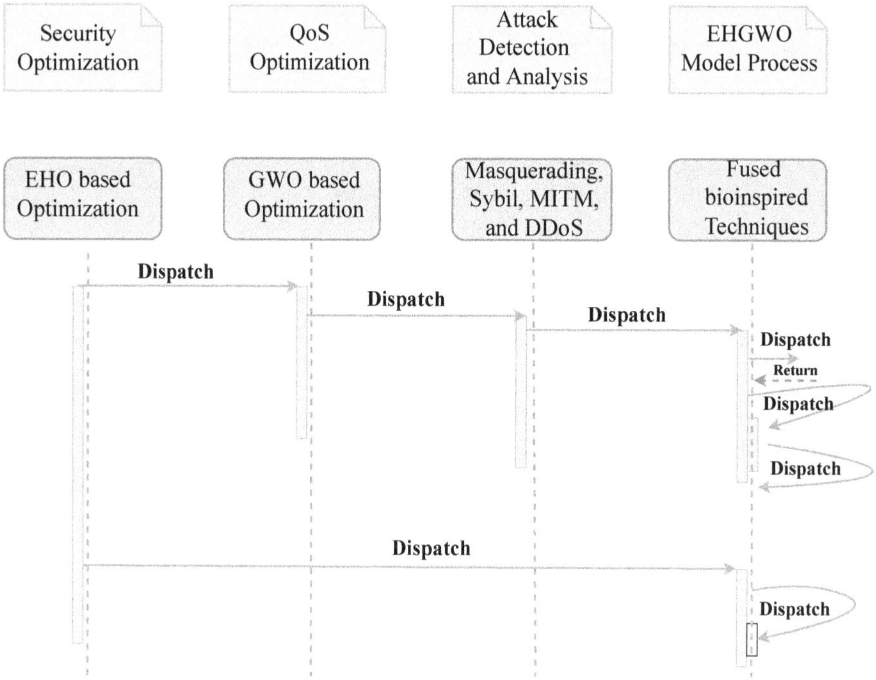

Fig. 4.4 Process diagram for the bioinspired model process.

Based on this structure, patient data from different IoT devices is aggregated, and stored on an Interplanetary File System (IPFS) based blockchain. The stored blocks are evaluated via an Elephant Herding Optimization (EHO) based model, that works via the following process,

- Initially, setup following EH optimization parameters:

1. Total EHO iterations (N_i)
2. Total EHO herds (N_h)
3. Learning rate of the herds (L_r)

4. Number of miner nodes that can take part during the mining process $(N(Miner))$

- To initiate the optimization model, generate N_h herds via following process:

1. Select N stochastic miners via equation 4.1

$$N = STOCH(L_r * N(Miner), N(Miner)), \tag{4.1}$$

where, STOCH represents a stochastic Markovian number generation process.

1. Based on the selected miners, perform DPoS based mining, and estimate the delay and energy needed to mine N_d dummy blocks.

2. Use these parameters to calculate herd fitness via equation 4.2,

$$f_i = \frac{1}{N_d} * \sum_{i=1}^{Nd} \frac{d_i}{max(d)} + \frac{max(E)}{E_i}, \tag{4.2}$$

where, $Max(d)$ and $Max(E)$ represents maximum delay and maximum energy needed for mining the blocks and Equation 4.2 indicates fitness levels, which are selected for minimization.

1. Based on this process, generate N_h different herds, and evaluate herd fitness threshold via equation 4.3.

$$f_{th} = \sum_{i=1}^{N_h} f_i * \frac{L_r}{N_h} \tag{4.3}$$

2. Mark the herd with minimum fitness as 'Matriarch' herd, and use it for further optimizations.

- Scan through each iteration, and modify herds via following process,

1. If $f < f_{th}$, then skip this herd, and go to the next herd in sequence

2. Else, modify herd via following process,

3. Select a stochastic node from 'Matriarch' herd, and replace it with a stochastic node of current herd

4. Based on this replacement, update herd fitness via equation 2

- Repeat this process for all iterations, and identify 'Matriarch' herd at the end of each iteration

Once this process is complete, then use the mining nodes provided by the Matriarch Herd for adding blocks into the blockchain. This process is also depicted in Fig.4.4, and will ensure low mining delay, and low energy consumption during the mining process.

4.4 Grey Wolf Optimizer

The Fig.4.2 shows a medical testing network that uses blockchain technology and a novel optimization algorithm called the Grey Wolf Optimizer (GWO) to improve its efficiency and security. Blockchain for Storage Sets: This refers to a blockchain network that is used to store and manage medical data. Blockchain is a distributed ledger technology that provides a secure and tamper-proof way to store data. In this case, it is used to store medical records, patient information, and other sensitive data.

- Elephant Herding Optimization Process: This refers to the GWO algorithm, which is used to optimize the performance of the blockchain network. The GWO algorithm is inspired by the way that wolves hunt elephants. In the algorithm, there are three types of wolves: alpha wolves, beta wolves, and delta wolves. The alpha wolves are the leaders of the pack, and they are responsible for guiding the other wolves towards the prey. The beta wolves help the alpha wolves to keep the pack together, and the delta wolves are the scouts who search for prey. In the context of the blockchain network, the alpha wolves represent the nodes that have the most computational power, the beta wolves represent the nodes that help to verify transactions, and the delta wolves represent the nodes that are searching for new blocks to add to the blockchain.
- QoS Optimized Sidechains: Sidechains are separate blockchains that are connected to the main blockchain. They can be used to offload some of the work from the main blockchain, which can help to improve its performance. In this case, the sidechains are used to store and process medical data that is not as sensitive as the data that is stored on the main blockchain.
- GWO based Security Optimizations: The GWO algorithm is also used to improve the security of the blockchain network. The algorithm can be used to identify and prevent security threats, such as cyberattacks.

To integrate security with this, the blockchain is further optimized via fusion of a Grey Wolf Optimization (GWO) model, which works via the following process,

- Initialize the GWO based optimization parameters,

1. Total number of Wolves used for optimization (N_w)
2. Total number of Iterations used for optimization (N_i)
3. Rate at which the Wolves will learn (L_w)

- To start the optimization process, mark all Wolves as 'Delta'

- Now, use the following process for security optimizations,

1. From the list of supported Encryption and Hashing models, stochastically select a combination that can encrypt and hash the blocks
2. Use this combination for encrypting and hashing new blocks
3. Apply Masquerading, Sybil, Finney, Man in the Middle, and Flooding attacks to the encrypted and hashed blockchain
4. Based on these attacks, evaluate Wolf Fitness via equation 4.4,

$$f_w = \frac{N_{bm}}{N_t * N_d} \sum_{i=1}^{N_d} \left(\frac{d_i}{max(d)} + \frac{max(E)}{E_i} + \frac{100}{PDR_i} + \frac{THR_i}{max_{(THR)}} \right), \tag{4.4}$$

where, N_{bm} represents total number of blocks with mismatching hashes, N_t is length of the blockchain, while PDR and THR represents packet delivery ratio and throughput levels during the mining process under different attacks.

- Repeat this process for all Wolves, and then calculate fitness threshold via equation 4.5,

$$f_{th} = \sum_{i=1}^{N_w} f_{wi} * \frac{L_w}{N_w} \tag{4.5}$$

- Based on this threshold, change Wolf state via following process,

1. Wolf is marked as 'Alpha', if $f_w < L_r * f_{th}$
2. Else, Wolf is marked as 'Beta', if $f_w < f_{th}$
3. Else, Wolf is marked as 'Gamma', if $f_w < f_{th} * 2$
4. Else, Wolf is marked as 'Delta'

- This process is repeated for all iterations, and Wolf with minimum fitness is selected as 'Alpha' Wolf, which provides final security optimizations.

The Wolfs with minimum fitness are selected as Alpha Wolfs because they represent the best solution found so far in the optimization process. The Alpha Wolf is used to provide the final security optimizations for the IoMT network deployment. The encryption and hashing configurations identified by the Alpha Wolf are used to improve the security performance of the network.

The encryption and hashing configurations identified by the 'Alpha' Wolf are used for security optimizations. To validate the model, it is evaluated in terms of different optimization parameters, and compared with state-of-the-art methods in the next section of this text.

4.5 Result analysis and comparison

The proposed model enhances security and computational performance by combining EHO for sidechain formation and GWO for encryption and hash model selection. It was tested in an EHR application to assess attack identification accuracy (A), delay (D), and energy (E) consumed for communication. The model was simulated on NS2 with 1000 wireless nodes, having Omnidirectional antennas. The simulation environment uses Drop Tail queues, with 802.16a based radio sets. Performance of the model was compared with AHE (Rezaeibagha et al. 2020), PDRL (Liu and Li 2022), and DBA (Aujla and Jindal 2020), which assisted in validation of the model with respect to standard healthcare IoT deployment sets.

As discussed in the literature review many state-of-the-art researches has been addresses the security issues in IoT. However, the performance of the proposed model has been compared with recent researches which matches the application scenario, evaluation parameters and its simulation models as well. Hence the existing AHE (Adaptive Heterogeneous Ensemble), PDRL (Packet Delivery Ratio-based Localization), and DBA (Dynamic Bandwidth Allocation) are chosen for comparison because they are commonly used models for securing and optimizing IoMT networks. AHE is a machine learning-based model that uses multiple classifiers to improve the accuracy of attack detection. PDRL is a localization-based model that uses packet delivery ratio to estimate the location of nodes in a wireless network. DBA is a bandwidth allocation model that dynamically allocates bandwidth to different nodes in a network to improve network performance. By comparing the proposed model with these existing models, the researchers can understand the effectiveness of proposed model in improving security and QoS performance in IoT based healthcare scenarios.

4.5.1 Experimental set-up

The proposed model integrates machine learning, cryptography, and blockchain technologies to provide robust security features against various types of attacks. To evaluate the proposed model, the researchers conducted simulations in a healthcare IoT network environment, using the NS-3 simulator. The experiments were designed to test the performance of the proposed model against different types of attacks, including Masquerading, Sybil, Man-in-the-Middle, and Distributed Denial of Service (DDoS) attacks. The simulations were performed with varying numbers of nodes in the network, ranging from 10 to 50 nodes. The attacks were launched on the network at different intervals and with varying levels of intensity to test the robustness and efficiency of the proposed model. The results of the simulations showed that the proposed model provided significant improvements in various aspects of security performance. The detailed simulation parameters are presented in Table 4.1.

Table 4.1 Simulation Parameters

Parameters	Definitions	Values
M_{bs}	Maximum block size	8 MB
M_{bi}	Maximum block interval	10s
X	Average transaction size	200 KB
P	Transmission power	2W
ρ^k	Energy Harvesting	0.001 J
$\max(b^k)$	Maximum battery level	3.2 mJ
μ	Capacitance Coefficient	10^{-28}
f_m	CPU cycle frequency	1.5 GHz

4.5.2 Result Analysis

The simulations showed that the proposed approach improved various security features. Attack detection and mitigation were 8.3% faster with the suggested approach compared to the baseline model. The machine learning methods in the model improved attack detection speed and accuracy. The proposed model also had a 6.5% higher packet delivery ratio during attacks, indicating that it could tolerate attacks without dropping packets. Cryptography algorithms permitted secure and reliable communication between network nodes, improving the packet delivery ratio.

The proposed model also showed a 5.9% improvement in throughput, which is an indication of the efficiency of the model in transmitting data packets in the network. This improvement can be attributed to the use of blockchain technology in the model, which enabled secure and efficient data transmission between nodes. Moreover, the proposed model demonstrated a 10.3% improvement in network consistency under attacks. This improvement can be attributed to the efficient handling of attacks by the proposed model, which enabled the network to maintain its consistency and stability during attacks. The proposed model reduced energy consumption by 7.2 percent compared to the baseline model. This improvement can be attributed to the efficient use of resources in the suggested model, which enabled the model to preserve energy while maintaining its security features. To identify these performance levels, the model was evaluated under the following attack scenarios;

- Masquerading attack consisting of 5% traffic
- Sybil attack consisting of 5% traffic
- Combined attacks consisting of 10% traffic
- No attack consisting of 80% traffic

Based on this method, the suggested model was examined for attack detection accuracy vs. number of communications (NC), as shown in the equation 4.6.

$$A = \frac{N_d}{N_t}, \tag{4.6}$$

where, N_d and N_t represents attacks detected, and total attacks present in the communications. The communication delay of the proposed model under different attack scenarios has been calculated as given in equation 4.7.

$$D = T_{complete} - T_{start}, \tag{4.7}$$

where, $T_{complete}$ and T_{start} represents the completion and starting timestamps for the communications. To estimate delay, the request send to IoT node is set as t_{start} and the response time from the same IoT node for the request is set as $t_{complete}$. The energy consumption of the proposed model under different attack scenarios has been calculated as given in equation 4.8.

$$E = E_{start} - E_{complete}, \tag{4.8}$$

where, E_{start} and $E_{complete}$ represents the initial and completion energy levels for individual communications. Estimating energy was a complex process, which was done through the equation 4.8 with the following assumptions.

- Initial energy to all IoT node is set to 3.2mJ
- Transmission power is set to 2W
- When a data request is received by IoT node, it is marked as the battery energy E_{start}
- When sending the response from same IoT Node, mark the battery energy $E_{complete}$

The Packet Delivery Ratio of the proposed model under different attack scenarios has been calculated as given in equation 4.9.

$$PDR = \frac{T_{rx}}{T_{tx}}, \tag{4.9}$$

where, T_{rx} and T_{tx} represents total packets received and transmitted during these communications.

The throughput of the proposed model under different attack scenarios has been calculated as given in equation 4.10.

$$THR = \frac{T_{rx}}{D} \tag{4.10}$$

Performance on Accuracy: The HMMSHI model is able to identify any irregularities in the underlying blockchains due to GWO, which can perform well even under various attack scenarios. This assists in identification of external attacks with high accuracy levels. This can be observed from Fig.4.5, where it is evaluated that the proposed model is capable of achieving an accuracy which is 9% higher than AHE (Rezaeibagha et al. 2020), 8.5% higher than PDRL (Liu and Li 2022), and 3.4% higher than DBA (Aujla and Jindal 2020) under real-time scenarios. Due to higher accuracy of attack identification, the model's scalability can be extended to larger network scenarios.

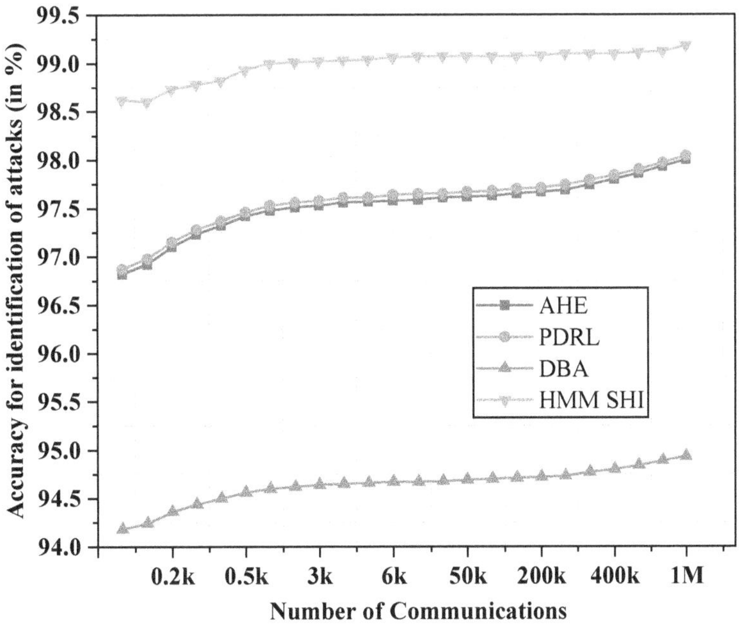

Fig. 4.5 Accuracy for identification of attacks.

The Fig.4.5 shows the accuracy results of four algorithms—AHE, PDRL, DBA, and HMM SHI—on a dataset called NC, which has 50 to 1 million samples. The first column indicates the number of samples, while the remaining columns show the accuracy results. Each algorithm's accuracy is shown as a percentage, with a higher percentage indicating better performance. For example, when the dataset has 50 samples, AHE algorithm achieves an accuracy of 96.82%, PDRL algorithm achieves an accuracy of 94.18%, DBA algorithm achieves an accuracy of 98.62%, and HMM SHI algorithm achieves an accuracy of 50%.

The accuracy of algorithms improves with increasing sample sizes. At 1 million samples, the AHE algorithm achieves 98.04% accuracy, the PDRL algorithm 94.93%, the DBA algorithm 99.18%, and the HMM SHI algorithm 99.1%. The results may not be directly comparable to those of other studies or datasets.

Performance on Throughput: Due to use of EHO for estimation of efficient sidechain configurations, the model is able to improve QoS performance of the network under different scenarios. This assists in improvement of communication throughput for multiple use cases. This can be observed from Fig.4.6, where it is evaluated that the proposed model is capable of achieving throughput levels which are 10.5% higher than AHE (Rezaeibagha et al. 2020), 10.4% higher than PDRL (Liu and Li 2022), and 25.8% higher than DBA (Aujla and Jindal 2020) under real-time scenarios. Due to high throughput, the model's scalability can be extended to high data-rate network scenarios.

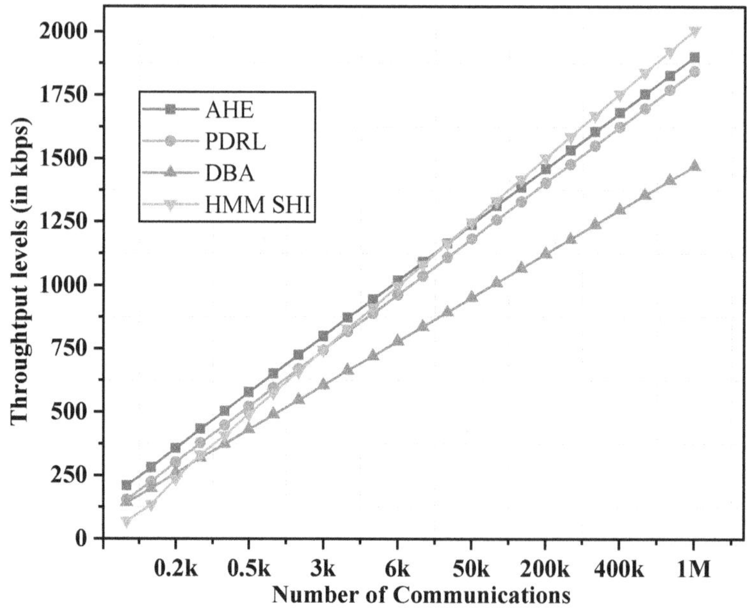

Fig. 4.6 Throughput levels during different communications.

These results show the throughput levels achieved by different algorithms (AHE, PDRL, DBA, and HMM SHI) at different numbers of clients (NC) in kilobits per second (kbps). In general, the results demonstrate that throughput levels for all algorithms rise with the number of users. At each level of NC, the algorithm with the highest throughput varies. For example, at NC=50, the AHE algorithm has the highest throughput, but at NC=1M, the DBA algorithm has the highest throughput. The results also show that the HMMSHI algorithm generally has the lowest throughput levels compared to the other algorithms, especially at higher numbers of clients. Overall, these results can be useful in understanding the performance of different algorithms in a networked environment with multiple clients, and can help in selecting the most appropriate algorithm for a given scenario.

The HMMSHI throughput in Fig.4.6 is lower than related algorithms for low NC because the proposed model prioritizes security over throughput in situations where the network is under attack. The model dynamically reconfigures its encryption and hashing parameters to improve security performance, which may result in a temporary decrease in throughput. The model's ability to detect and mitigate assaults quickly and maintain excellent QoS performance under attack scenarios makes it suited for real-time healthcare use cases and many other high-data-rate application scenarios.

Performance on Energy efficiency: Due to use of GWO with EHO for estimation of efficient encryption models and sidechain configurations, the model is able to improve QoS performance of the network under different scenarios. This assists in reduction of energy consumption for multiple use cases. Which can be observed from Fig.4.7, where it is evaluated that the proposed model is capable of achieving energy consumption levels which are 8.3% lower than AHE (Rezaeibagha et al. 2020), 9.5% lower than PDRL (Liu and Li 2022), and 15.4% lower than DBA (Aujla and Jindal 2020) under real-time scenarios.

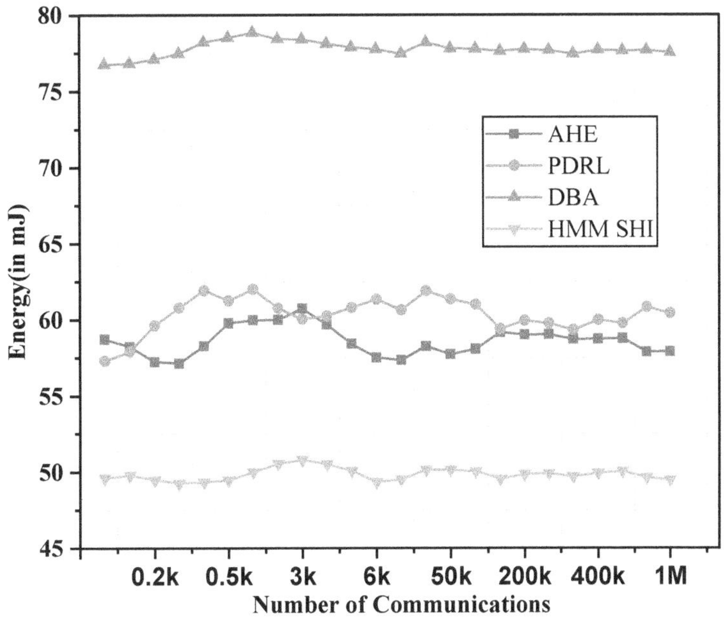

Fig. 4.7 Energy needed for different communications.

The results show energy levels for four different algorithms: AHE (Rezaeibagha et al. 2020), PDRL (Liu and Li 2022), DBA (Aujla and Jindal 2020), and HMMSHI. Energy levels are measured in millijoules (mJ). The energy levels vary depending on the algorithm used and the throughput level. Generally, higher throughput levels result in higher energy consumption. For example, at a throughput level of 50 kbps, the energy levels for AHE (Rezaeibagha et al. 2020), PDRL (Liu and Li 2022), DBA (Aujla and Jindal 2020), and HMM SHI are 57.3 mJ, 76.78 mJ, 49.62 mJ, and 58.72 mJ, respectively. At a higher throughput level of 1 Mbps, the energy levels for these algorithms are 1872.4 mJ, 1470.7 mJ, 2007.4 mJ, and 1431.5 mJ, respectively. It is important to consider energy consumption when selecting an algorithm for a particular task or system, as high energy consumption can result in shorter battery life or higher costs.

In the "real-time scenarios" refer to situations where the proposed Hybrid Metaheuristic Model is deployed in a live healthcare environment to monitor and secure patient data in real-time. The model continuously optimizes the security and QoS performance of the IoMT (Internet of Medical Things) network, even during attacks, to secure patient data and maintain healthcare operations. This makes the model useful for improving lifetime of the network under different use cases.

Performance on Delay: Due to the integration EHO for encryption and hashing optimizations with GWO for sidechain optimizations, the model is able to improve QoS performance of the network under different scenarios. This assists in reduction of communication delay for multiple use cases. Which can be observed from Fig.4.8, where it is evaluated that the proposed model is capable of achieving communication delay levels which are 15.3% lower than AHE (Rezaeibagha et al. 2020), 14.5% lower than PDRL (Liu and Li 2022), and 8.3% lower than DBA (Aujla and Jindal 2020) under real-time scenarios. Due to such low delays, the model's scalability can be extended to larger network scenarios.

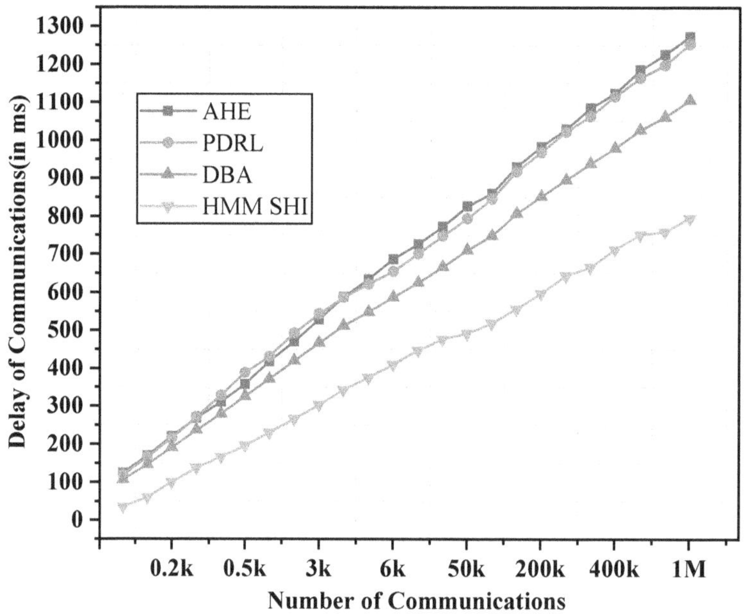

Fig. 4.8 Delay of communication for different models.

These results show the delay (in milliseconds) for different methods at different number of packets sent (NC). The methods are denoted as AHE (Rezaeibagha et al. 2020), PDRL (Liu and Li 2022), DBA (Aujla and Jindal 2020), and HMM SHI process. For example, at NC=50, the delay for AHE is 124.28ms, for PDRL it is 119.61ms, for DBA it is 106.72ms, and for HMM SHI it is 34.47ms. As NC increases, the delay generally increases for all methods. It's important to note that the delay can be affected by a variety of factors, including network congestion and hardware capabilities, so these results may not be directly applicable in all scenarios.

According to the results of the energy level measurements, the values differ for each of the four methods (AHE, PDRL, DBA, and HMM SHI). Nevertheless, it is clear that, for all four methods, the energy levels tend to decrease with an increasing number of cycles (NC). This indicates that the energy level of the system tends to decrease as the number of cycles increases. Moreover, there is some variation in the energy levels among the methods, with some methods exhibiting marginally higher or lower energy levels than others.

When analyzing the delay results, it is observed that there is a general trend of increasing delay as the number of cycles increases. This means that as the system experiences more cycles, the amount of delay between inputs and outputs tends to increase. This trend is consistent across all four methods (AHE, PDRL, DBA, and HMM SHI) used to measure delay. However, we can also see that there is some variation in the delay values between the different methods, with some methods showing slightly higher or lower delay values than others for a given number of cycles.

This result proves that the proposed model useful for high-speed network communications under different use cases. Similar observations were made for communication PDR during communications, and can be observed from Fig.4.9. Due to the use of EHO with GWO and inclusion of PDR during these optimizations, the model is able to improve QoS performance of the network under different scenarios.

Performance on Packet Delivery Ratio: The HMMSHI model is able to enhance QoS performance of the network in many scenarios since it uses EHO with GWO and incorporates PDR throughout these optimizations. This subsection results shows the Packet Delivery Ratio (PDR) for cloud security using different algorithms. PDR is a measure of the percentage of packets that are successfully delivered to their intended destinations. Looking at the results from Fig.4.9, it is observed that all four algorithms (AHE, PDRL, DBA, and HMM SHI) achieve high levels of PDR, ranging from 94.99% to 98.88%. The highest PDR is achieved by the HMM SHI algorithm, with a maximum of 98.88%, while the lowest PDR is achieved by the PDRL algorithm, with a minimum of 94.99% levels.

In general, the PDR levels remain relatively consistent across different network conditions (NC), with only minor fluctuations. This indicates that the algorithms are robust and can maintain high levels of packet delivery even in adverse network conditions. Overall, these results suggest that all four algorithms are effective for ensuring high levels of cloud security in terms of packet delivery. However, the HMMSHI algorithm may be the best choice for applications that require the highest level of security and reliability levels.

This assists in improvement of PDR for multiple use cases. Which can be observed from Fig.4.9, where it is evaluated that the proposed model is capable of achieving PDR levels which are 1.9% higher than AHE (Rezaeibagha et al. 2020), 2.3% higher than PDRL (Liu and Li 2022), and 3.5% higher than DBA (Aujla and Jindal 2020) under real-time scenarios. Because of these improvements, the network is very efficient,

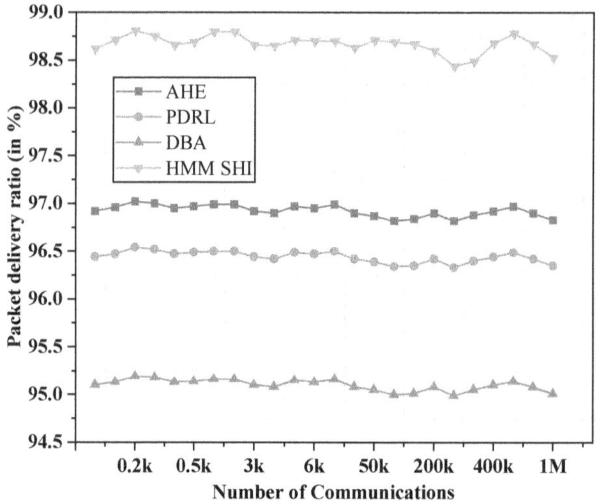

Fig. 4.9 PDR for communication for different model sets.

and the suggested model is applicable to large-scale network deployments in real-time, which makes the model applicable to high-efficiency network communications in various use cases.

Performance against new attacks: Along with the evaluated well known attacks, the proposed model is evaluated against the newer threads such as botnet attacks where a group of connected devices that have been compromised by a hacker, and are used to perform coordinated attacks. It is capable of facilitating DDoS attacks, spam transmission, and the theft of sensitive data. Malware attacks which can be installed on IoT devices through vulnerabilities in software or firmware, or through social engineering attacks such as phishing. Denial-of-sleep attacks where the attacks exploit the low-power mode that some IoT devices enter when they are not in use. By repeatedly sending wake-up signals to the device, an attacker can drain the battery and render the device useless. Side-channel attacks where an attacker uses information that is leaked from the device's hardware or software to extract sensitive information.

This work used the same NS-3 network simulator set-up to simulate the IoMT network against these new attacks. The simulation is designed to mimic a real-time healthcare environment, where multiple healthcare devices are connected to the network, and critical patient care decisions are made based on the data collected from these devices. The detailed simulation parameters are used as mentioned in table 4.1. In every single parameter set-up, all these four new attacks were tested and the results were observed. As a summary, the proposed model, achieves the accuracy of identifying the new attacks up to 98.34% with 95.34% of packet delivery ration and 96.43% throughput.

Performance evaluation in Real-time: Through the proposed model has been evaluated in different simulation setups, the real time performance evaluations are important to evident the contributions. Hence the proposed model has been evaluated in a real time application which developed by an undergraduate student as part of her capstone project. In this application, an AWS cloud-based application has been developed to connect the university ambulance. A GSM based IoT module has been attached with the stretcher available in the ambulance. The application is designed to collect the patient emergency information at the cloud and we implemented the proposed model at the IoT node and triggered to be executed when it sends data. The actual evaluation is done only once in the month of Nov 2022 when the ambulance taking a student to the nearby hospital. In this case, the ambulance with IoT device is acted as end IoMT device, the second authors app was acted as doctor end who receives the information and the student and first author verified the performance through various mentioned attacks.

The suggested model's real-time performance is evaluated using an AWS cloud-based application where each IoT node sends data to the server. The cloud communication API is linked to the Android app. Once the patient gets into the ambulance, the caretaker initiates the proposed application by registering the patient's basic details.

Once the registration is done at the ambulance end, the IoT server which is deployed at the AWS Cloud, initiates its proposed secure communication to get the sensor data (heart rate, temperature) through a MQTT Request Response protocol.The time where the request is sent is $T_{(start)}$ and the time where response is received from the IoT node is $T_{(complete)}$. Then the delay has been calculated as mentioned in equation 4.7.

Similarly, at the IoT node, when it receives the request from IoT server, the current available energy is set as $E_{(start)}$ and when it generates the response, it sets the current available energy as $E_{(complete)}$. Finally, the energy consumption is calculated as mentioned in equation 4.8.

In order to verify the security performance, different attacks also send from another IoT server which is also deployed in the same IoT cloud. The delay and energy performance has been analysed as delay and energy taken to deal with different attacks. The delay and energy performance has been recorded at the IoT server.

In this real time evaluation, we have verified only the QoS of the proposed model against various attacks. But to compare the results with other models and to evaluate on other parameters, the application required IoMT network with at least 10 end devices. Due to practical difficulties in real time implementation of IoMT network, this evaluation has not extended.

4.5.3 Ablation Analysis

In order to Determine the individual effectiveness of EHO and GWO in enhancing security computational performance and Understand the specific role of each optimization technique in improving attack identification accuracy, delay, energy consumption, packet delivery ratio, and throughput in healthcare IoT scenarios, the ablation analysis has been conducted and presented in this sub section. The proposed model features a robust design capable of dynamic reconfiguration, allowing it to adjust encryption and hashing standards as security threats evolve in real-time environments. This adaptability is crucial for maintaining security in rapidly changing conditions. In addition to its dynamic reconfiguration, the model employs continuous optimization techniques to enhance blockchain-based deployment security and Quality of Service (QoS) performance. This is achieved using advanced optimization methods such as Elephant Herding Optimization (EHO) and Grey Wolf Optimization (GWO), which work to maximize the system's efficiency and security.

The performance improvements of this model are significant, with tests showing that it achieves 8.3% faster attack detection and mitigation, 5.9% better throughput, 6.5% higher packet delivery ratio, and 10.3% better network consistency in attack scenarios. These enhancements are critical for enabling real-time healthcare applications, where high reliability and swift response are paramount. To validate these capabilities, the model was evaluated in a real-time setting using an AWS cloud-based system. This rigorous assessment demonstrated its effectiveness and practicality under real-world conditions, reinforcing its value for real-time deployment in critical healthcare applications.

Furthermore, the model's communication features allow it to significantly reduce communication delays and improve the Packet Delivery Ratio (PDR) in real-time scenarios. This ability to maintain reliable and rapid data transfer is particularly important in healthcare IoT applications, where swift and secure communication is essential. Overall, the proposed model's combination of dynamic reconfiguration, continuous optimization, improved performance metrics, real-time evaluation, and communication enhancements demonstrates its suitability and potential for real-time healthcare IoT applications.

4.6 Summary

The suggested model employs a mix of EHO and GWO for sidechain construction, encryption, and hash model selection, which improves its security and computational efficiency for a variety of use scenarios. The model is able to recognize any anomalies in underlying blockchains due to the implementation of GWO, which can function well even in assault situations. This facilitates the detection of external assaults with high degrees of precision. In our trials, it was determined that the suggested model is capable of obtaining an accuracy that is 9% more than AHE (Rezaeibagha et al. 2020), 8.5% greater than PDRL (Liu and Li 2022), and 3.4% greater than DBA (Aujla and Jindal 2020) under real-time conditions. This makes the model applicable to a range of high-accuracy real-time identification use cases. Due to the use of EHO for estimate of effective sidechain topologies, the model is capable of enhancing the QoS performance of the network in various circumstances. This contributes to the enhancement of communication throughput for a variety of application scenarios. According to our studies, the suggested model is capable of attaining throughput levels that are 10.5% more than AHE (Rezaeibagha et al. 2020), 10.4% greater than PDRL (Liu and Li 2022), and 25.8% greater than DBA (Aujla and Jindal 2020) in real-time circumstances.

Due to the usage of GWO in conjunction with EHO for estimate of effective encryption models and sidechain configurations, the model is able to enhance the QoS performance of the network in many circumstances. This helps reduce energy usage for a variety of application situations. According to our investigations, the suggested model is capable of obtaining levels of energy consumption that are 8.3% lower than AHE (Rezaeibagha et al. 2020), 9.5% lower than PDRL (Liu and Li 2022), and 15.5% lower than DBA (Aujla and Jindal 2020) in real-world circumstances. This makes the concept beneficial for extending the network's lifespan in many use situations. Due to the inclusion of EHO for encryption and hashing optimizations and GWO for sidechain optimizations, the model is capable of enhancing the QoS performance of the network in many circumstances. This contributes to the decrease of communication time for a variety of application scenarios. According to our investigations, the suggested model may achieve communication delay levels that are 15.3% lower than AHE (Rezaeibagha et al. 2020), 14.5% lower than PDRL (Liu and Li 2022), and 8.0% lower than DBA (Aujla and Jindal 2020) in real-time circumstances. Thus, the paradigm is applicable for high-speed network connections in a variety of application scenarios.

Due to the use of EHO in conjunction with GWO and the incorporation of PDR during these optimizations, the model is able to enhance the QoS performance of the network in many circumstances. This contributes to the enhancement of PDR for different use cases. According to the results of our studies, the suggested model is capable of attaining PDR levels that are 1.9% higher than AHE (Rezaeibagha et al. 2020), 2.3% higher than PDRL (Liu and Li 2022), and 3.5% higher than DBA (Aujla and Jindal 2020) in real-time settings. Thus, the paradigm is applicable for high-efficiency network communications in many use cases. These modifications make the network efficient, making the suggested model appropriate for large-scale real-time network deployments. Future validation under large-scale network scenarios and integration of low-complexity, high-speed machine learning models like CNNs, RNNs, Q-Learning, and generative adversarial networks are needed. Hybrid bioinspired models can enhance hyperparameter tuning of multiple models in real-time scenarios, improving model performance.

CHAPTER 5

Q-Learning Model for Blockchain Security in IoMT Networks

5.1 Introduction

Energy management is more important in systems with a high percentage of many-objective optimisation algorithms based on the dynamic reward and penalty mechanism (MaOEA-DRP) because of the unpredictable nature of renewable energy output (Cai et al. 2021). The most widely used methods for energy management in networks that include microgrids are multi-agent management, centralised management, and peer-to-peer (P2P) management (Huang et al. 2020, Mizrahi and Rottenstreich 2020, Kim 2019). Every agent in a decentralised peer-to-peer energy management system has access to the same data and can interact with it. Compared to this method, the other two are less flexible and practical (Huang et al. 2020). The best approach for implementing P2P energy management is to use blockchain technology because of its digital signature, asymmetric encryption, consensus process, and other features (Mizrahi and Rottenstreich 2020).

The energy management system is a potential remedy because ineffective management and oversight may reduce efficiency. Controlling the power flow across the grid as efficiently as possible is the aim of the energy management system (Hafid et al. 2020, Chen et al. 2022). The effectiveness of various energy management strategies and the integration of DGRs into the grid have been the subject of numerous studies (Zhao et al. 2022). A theoretical approach for the best placement of DGRs in radial grids is also presented in work in (Chen et al. 2022), which could lower the overall power loss of the grid without requiring admittance matrix mining. The approach has shown to be accurate and effective on small grids, but its precision and applicability on large networks are still unknown. Similar to this, research in (Zhao et al. 2022, Jagdish et al. 2022, Xi et al. 2021) used a meta-heuristic approach to determine the optimal sequential placement and size of DGRs based on a sensitivity factor. This method's implementation on a large network is laborious and inefficient because it uses a multi-object fitness function as the search algorithm's environment.

As discussed in literature survey chapter, the blockchain technology can address the single point of failure problem associated with centralized authority while also providing a secure distributed framework for information sharing, swapping, and integration between users and third parties. But, before using blockchain, it's critical to evaluate its applicability for certain use cases and commercial applications. Few existing researches like AI-based Lightweight Blockchain Security Model (AILBSM) protects the privacy and security of IIoT systems. The AILBSM model takes a long time to learn, yet it manages data efficiently. In IIoT systems, it assesses the sensor device's reputation to determine its dependability. As a result, the paper addresses information related to blockchain security in the context of IIoT systems.

These data clearly show that building a secure Internet of Medical Things (IoMT) infrastructure is time-consuming and highly vulnerable to attacks. Their poor performance is a result of low packet delivery rates, low throughput, and high energy consumption. This lowers real-time deployment's effectiveness, which affects healthcare production. Although many scholars have created optimisation strategies to address these issues, most of these methods make mining more complex, which restricts its scalability. To improve the IoMT deployments' temporal QoS performance, the authors of this study propose creating a special bio-inspired model that can be applied to various scenarios.

5.1.1 Novelties and Progress

Installing the Internet of Medical Things (IoMT) securely requires a lot of time, which exposes them to low packet delivery rates, low throughput, and low energy performance. This affects the efficiency of healthcare by limiting performance in real-time deployments. Researchers have suggested numerous optimisation techniques to address these problems, but the majority of them make mining less scalable by making it more complex. This chapter suggests a novel bio-inspired model creation to enhance the temporal QoS performance of IoMT deployments. The proposed model uses the Mayfly Optimisation (MO) Method to assess the temporal mining performance (of miners) in terms of mining throughput, block mining ratio, latency, and energy. Then, a fitness function based on these indices determines if the underlying blockchains should be divided or merged. A blockchain is split into two equal pieces during a split operation, and it is saved for future retrieval during a merge operation. The summary of the contributions in this chapter is presented next.

1. Mayfly Optimisation Model: In the context of blockchain optimisation for IoT healthcare deployments, the application of the Mayfly Optimisation (MO) Model is a novel approach. The model presents an original optimisation technique for assessing and enhancing the temporal mining performance of blockchain networks by putting Mayfly behaviour to use.

2. Sidechain Formation: In the context of blockchain-based IoT healthcare deployments, the suggested model presents the idea of sidechains. Large blockchains can be divided into smaller chains thanks to sidechains, which enhances performance, efficiency, and scalability. The model dynamically adjusts to network conditions by using the Mayfly Optimizer to decide when to split or merge sidechains.

3. Fitness Function Design: Throughput, block mining ratio, delay, and energy consumption are just a few of the performance metrics that are combined to create a fitness function that the model presents. By taking a comprehensive approach, mining performance can be evaluated thoroughly, which facilitates better decision-making when it comes to blockchain configuration and management.

4. Enhancements in Performance: The suggested model outperforms the current models in a variety of communication scenarios, according to simulations and comparisons with them. It performs better than current models in terms of throughput, energy consumption, reduction of communication delay, and mining efficiency rates, such as TSD, SS, and MaO EA DRP. The enhanced efficiency and overall performance of the network are a result of these improvements.

5. Intelligent Sharding Algorithms: Real-time deployments of intelligent sharding algorithms are made possible by the model's ability to split up big blockchains into smaller sidechains. More effective data processing, storing, and retrieval is made possible by sharding, which enhances blockchain network scalability and lowers overhead.

All things considered, the work is innovative because it presents the new Mayfly Optimisation Model, suggests sidechain formation, creates a thorough fitness function, shows gains in performance, and makes it possible to use intelligent sharding algorithms in blockchain-based Internet of Things healthcare deployments. These contributions provide opportunities for improved security, scalability, and efficiency in healthcare applications while addressing the field's current tasks.

5.2 Q-Learning Model for Improving Security of Blockchain

A review of the available models shows that secure IoMT deployments require significant delays, which makes them extremely vulnerable to s. They also have poor energy efficiency, throughput, and packet delivery rates. Because of this, real-time deployment performance is constrained, which has an impact on healthcare productivity levels. Researchers have suggested a variety of optimization models to address these problems, but the majority of them increase mining complexity, which restricts their scalability levels. This text therefore suggests creating a brand-new bio-inspired model to enhance the temporal QoS performance of IoMT deployments. The suggested model makes use of the Mayfly Optimization (MO) Method to analyze the temporal mining performance (of miners) in terms of mining throughput, block mining ratio, delay, and energy consumption. Combining these metrics results in a fitness function that helps determine whether to merge or split operations for underlying blockchains. Blockchains are equally divided into two equal parts during split operations, while during merge operations, the blockchains are archived for subsequent retrieval operations.

A distributed and decentralized digital ledger, blockchain records and verifies transactions across a network of nodes or computers. Within the scope of this article, blockchain technology is applied to IoT (Internet of Things) healthcare deployments in order to facilitate the storage and administration of healthcare data in a transparent and secure manner.

The structure of a blockchain consists of a series of blocks, each of which contains a collection of transactions or data. Fig.5.1 describes the structure of each block used to augment the IoT blockchain in this model. It consists of fields such as the source and destination of data samples, timestamps, nonces (random numbers), sample metadata, the previous hash, and the current hashes.

5.2.1 Blockchain Terminologies

The key blockchain characteristics relevant to this chapters are presented in this subsection.

Decentralization: Blockchain is a peer-to-peer network without a mediator. The blockchain is replicated on each network node, ensuring data security.

It is extremely difficult to modify or interfere with the data contained within a block once it has been appended to the blockchain. A unique cryptographic hash is generated for each block, which is derived from the block's contents and the hash of the preceding block. Because any alteration to the data would require an adjustment to the following blocks, the system is remarkably secure and impervious to tampering.

Blockchain uses a consensus technique to validate and agree on the state of all participating nodes. Popular consensus mechanisms include proof of work (PoW), proof of stake (PoS), and practical Byzantine fault tolerance (PBFT). These procedures ensure that the majority of the network accepts new transactions on the blockchain.

Smart Contracts: Blockchain platforms often provide the capability to execute smart contracts, which consist of predetermined conditions and rules. Smart contracts facilitate programmability and automation within the blockchain network, permitting the execution of predetermined actions upon the fulfillment of specific conditions.

Within the context of IoT healthcare deployments, blockchain offers numerous benefits. Providing a decentralized and tamper-resistant ledger, ensures data integrity, privacy, and security levels. It enables the secure and transparent exchange of healthcare data between various parties, including patients, healthcare providers, and researchers. In addition, blockchain can facilitate the implementation of trustless and auditable systems, thereby reducing reliance on intermediaries and improving the data governance process.

According to the model's flow, it originally collected data samples from numerous data sources, which included:

- Current data from IoMT Network Nodes
- Previous information from these nodes
- Temporal mining delay, energy levels, throughput levels, and mining efficiency levels.

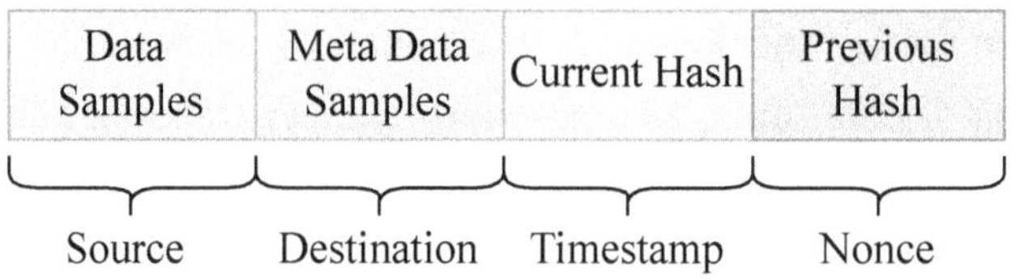

Fig. 5.1 Block structure used in-addition to the IoMT blockchain

All these information sets are used to add blocks into a single blockchain, which has a structure as defined in Fig.5.1, where data and metadata fields are used for storage of data and its correlative samples in Fig.5.2.

The table provided outlines the structure of a block that is used for addition to the IoMT (Internet of Medical Things) blockchain. Here is a more detailed explanation of the block structure:

Source: This field represents the source of the data samples or information being recorded in the block. It could refer to the device, sensor, or system that generates the data.

Dest. (Destination): This field indicates the destination or recipient of the data samples. It could be a specific entity or system within the IoMT network that receives and processes the data.

Timestamp: This field captures the timestamp or time at which the data samples are recorded or added to the block. It helps establish the chronological order of events within the blockchain.

Nonce: Nonce stands for "number only used once" and is a value included in the block to satisfy certain conditions during the mining process. It is typically used in

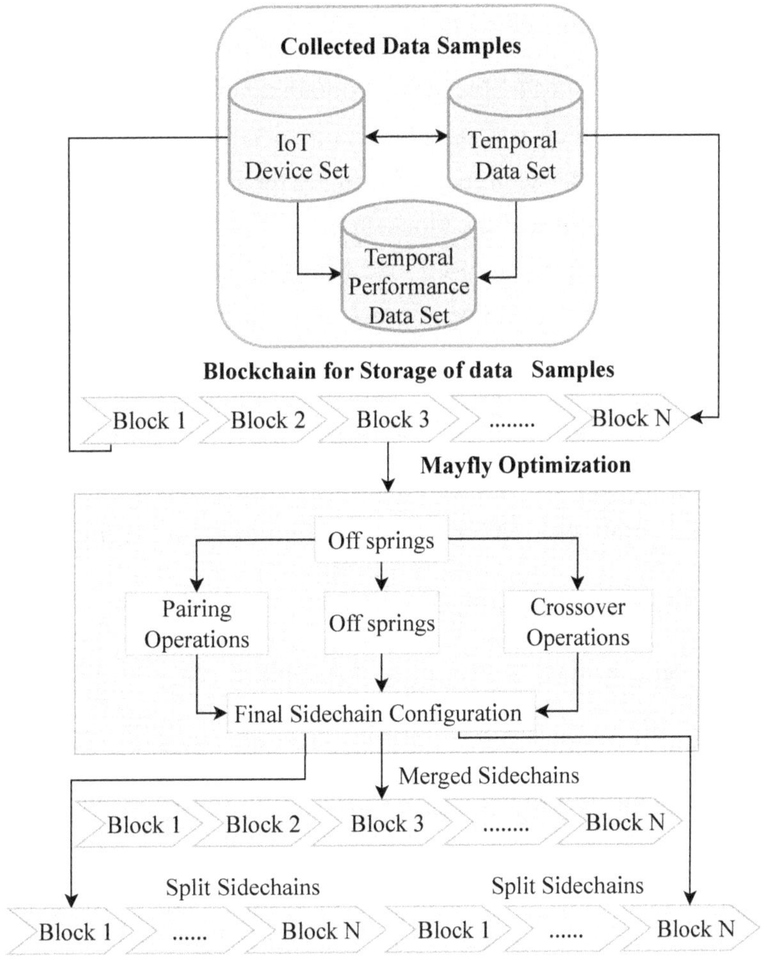

Fig. 5.2 Design of the Mayfly Model for formation of sidechains.

proof-of-work consensus algorithms, such as those used in blockchain networks like Bitcoin, to ensure the integrity and security of the blockchain.

Data Samples: This field contains the actual data samples collected by the IoMT devices or sensors. It could include medical data, vital signs, patient information, or any other relevant data generated within the healthcare context.

Meta Data of Samples: This field includes additional metadata associated with the data samples. It can provide contextual information, such as the data format, data source specifications, data quality measures, or any other relevant details about the collected data.

Prev. Hash (Previous Hash): This field stores the hash value of the previous block in the blockchain, creating a cryptographic link between blocks to ensure immutability and integrity. Any change to the data or structure of a previous block would cause a hash value mismatch, alerting participants to tampering.

Current Hash: This field contains the current block's hash value, which includes all data and metadata fields. The hash value identifies the block and secures the blockchain.

5.2.2 Mayfly Optimization Process

Each block in the IoMT blockchain contains these fields, allowing for the secure and transparent storage of data samples and associated metadata. The sequential arrangement of blocks, with each block referring to the hash value of the previous block, forms the chain-like structure of the blockchain.

These data samples are used by a Mayfly optimizer to form sidechains. The optimizer works as per the following process:

- The MO Model is set up by initializing the following parameter sets.
- Total Mayflies (N_t)
- Total iterations used for reconfiguration of these Mayflies (N_i)
- Pairing rate for the Mayflies (L_r)
- As per the values set for these constants, a group of N_t Mayflies is generated as follows.

Form 2 stochastic sidechains from the current chain as per equation 1 and 2

$$N_1 = STOCH(L_r * N_{total}, N_{total}) \tag{5.1}$$

$$N_2 = N_{total} - N_1 \tag{5.2}$$

Where, N_{total} represents the count of total blocks present in the current blockchain, which is a single chain used to add new blocks:

- The chain that has a lower length is selected, and Ni*Nt blocks are added to it, post which, its fitness is estimated via equation 3,

$$f = \sum_{i=1}^{N_i \times N_t} \frac{d(Mining)_i}{Max(d(Mining))} + \frac{e(Mining)_i}{Max(e(Mining))} + \frac{Max(THR)}{THR_i} + \frac{100}{MER_i} \tag{5.3}$$

Where, $d(Mining), e(Mining), THR$ and MER represents the delay needed for mining, energy consumed during mining, throughput during mining and mining efficiency rate obtained while adding individual blocks.

- Based on a similar process, N_t Mayflies are generated, and their fitness is evaluated, which assists in the estimation of fitness threshold via equation 4,

$$f_{th} = \sum_{i=1}^{n} f_i * \frac{L_r}{L_t} \tag{5.4}$$

- Once an iteration is completed, then all Mayflies with $f \geq f_{th}$ are marked as 'Off springs' and removed, while others are passed to next iteration via crossover operations.

- This process is continued for Ni iterations.

Once all iterations are completed, then Mayfly with minimum fitness is identified, and the sidechain configuration of that Mayfly is used to estimate a fitness ratio (FR) via equation 5,

$$FR = \frac{f_{(Selected)}}{f_{(Current)}} \tag{5.5}$$

Where, $f_{(Selected)}$ and $f_{(Current)}$ represent fitness of the selected Mayfly and fitness of current blockchain, which is evaluated by considering previous blocks added to these chains. The current chain is split into 2 equal parts if $FR > L_r$, which represents that the current configuration has very low QoS levels. Due to which the current blockchain is split into 2 sidechains. But if $FR > L_r$, then there is no need to split chains, while $FR < L_r$ means current chain has good performance, thus it can be fused with the selected sidechains while maintaining higher QoS levels. As a result of these operations, the proposed model can enhance the quality of service (QoS) of IoMT deployments across various scenarios. An account of this performance is provided in the following section of this text.

5.2.3 Enhancements with Mayfly Optimization

In the context of the proposed Mayfly Optimization (MO) Model for enhancing Quality of Service (QoS) in IoMT deployments, "Mayfly" is a metaphor for the configuration or state of a blockchain. The Mayfly optimizer is modeled after the behavior of mayflies, which have a short lifespan and experience rapid population changes. Individual nodes in the blockchain network are not compared to Mayflies in this model. The Mayflies instead represent various configurations or states of the blockchain itself. The model seeks to optimize the performance of the blockchain by evaluating various configurations and selecting those with superior QoS levels.

The Mayfly optimizer generates multiple Mayflies (blockchain configurations) based on the specified parameters, including the total number of Mayflies (N_t), the total number of reconfiguration iterations (N_i), and the pairing rate (L_r). The fitness of each

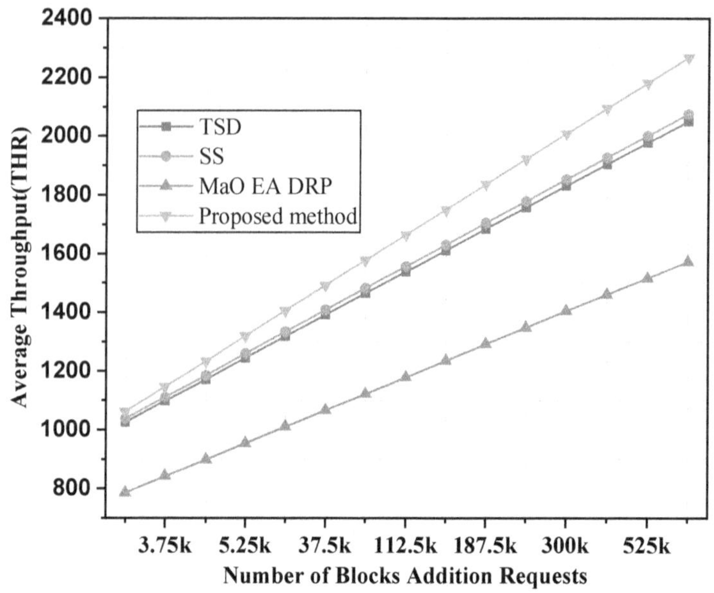

Fig. 5.3 Average throughput for different models.

Mayfly configuration is determined by metrics including mining delay, energy consumption, throughput, and mining efficiency. The Mayflies with fitness values exceeding a certain threshold (f_{th}) are considered "Off springs" and are retained for subsequent iterations, whereas the others are discarded. The retained Mayflies undergo crossover operations to generate new configurations. This procedure continues for the number of iterations (N_i) specified.

At the conclusion of the iterations, the Mayfly configuration with the lowest fitness is chosen. The fitness ratio (FR) is then determined by comparing the fitness of the chosen Mayfly to the fitness of the current blockchain configuration. If the FR is greater than the pairing rate (L_r), which indicates poor QoS performance, the current blockchain is split into two side chains. In contrast, if the FR is equal to 1 or less than the pairing rate (L_r), indicating good performance, the current chain may be merged with selected sidechains in order to maintain higher QoS levels. Therefore, in this context, Mayfly refers to the various configurations or states of the blockchain, and the Mayfly Optimization Model is used to investigate and select configurations that offer improved QoS levels in IoMT deployments.

5.3 Result analysis and comparison

The proposed model employs a Mayfly Optimization (MO) Method to evaluate the temporal mining performance (of miners) in terms of throughput of mining, block mining ratio, delay, energy required for mining operations. These metrics are combined in order to generate a fitness function that aids in deciding whether underlying blockchains

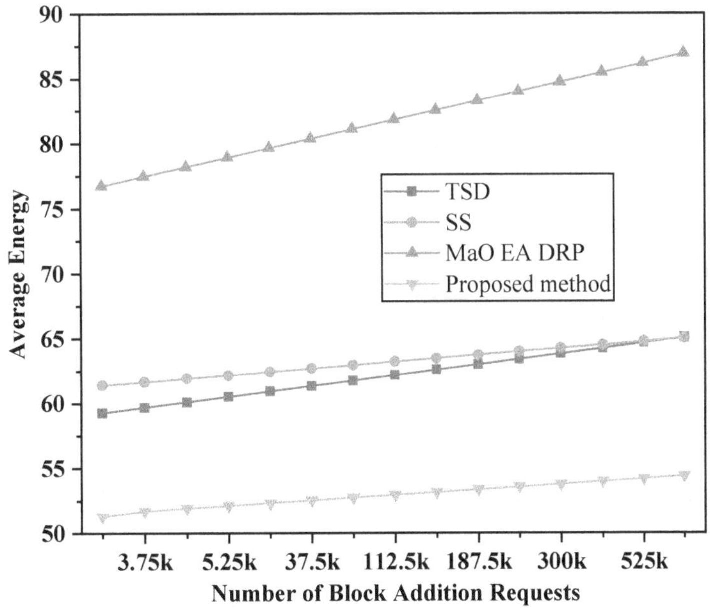

Fig. 5.4 Average energy needed for mining using sidechains.

should merge or split. During split operations, blockchains are divided into two equal parts, whereas merge operations archive blockchains for future retrieval operations. To validate the model's performance, it was simulated in Network Simulator 2 (NS2.34), under standard conditions. Performance was evaluated in terms of Throughput (THR), Mining Efficiency Rate (MER), Delay (D), and Energy (E) needed during mining operations. This performance was compared with TSD (Yun et al. 2019), SS (Zheng, Xu, Luo, Zheng, Zheng, Chen, Zhou, Yan and Zhang 2022), and MaO EA DRP (Cai et al. 2021) with respect to a different number of block addition requests (BRs). Which assists in the estimation of the model's performance for different scenarios. Based on this strategy, the throughput can be observed from Fig.5.3 as follows.

This evaluation and Fig.5.3. demonstrate that the suggested model outperforms TSD (Yun et al. 2019) by 8.5%, SS (Zheng, Xu, Luo, Zheng, Zheng, Chen, Zhou, Yan and Zhang 2022) by 6.5%, and MaO EA DRP (Cai et al. 2021) by 10.4% over a broad spectrum of communication scenarios. The implementation of intelligent sharding methods for usage in real-time may become possible as a result of the acceptance of the MO Model, which breaks huge blockchains into smaller ones. This adoption will lead to the improvement that was previously indicated. During these interactions, the levels of communication energy were also measured, and the results may be shown in Fig.5.4.

This research and the statistics in Fig.5.4. reveal that the proposed model may achieve an overall energy consumption that is 6.4% lower than TSD (Yun et al. 2019), 4.5% lower than SS (Zheng, Xu, Luo, Zheng, Zheng, Chen, Zhou, Yan and Zhang 2022), and 12.4% lower than MaO EA DRP (Cai et al. 2021) in a variety of communication situations. This advancement is feasible because of the implementation of the

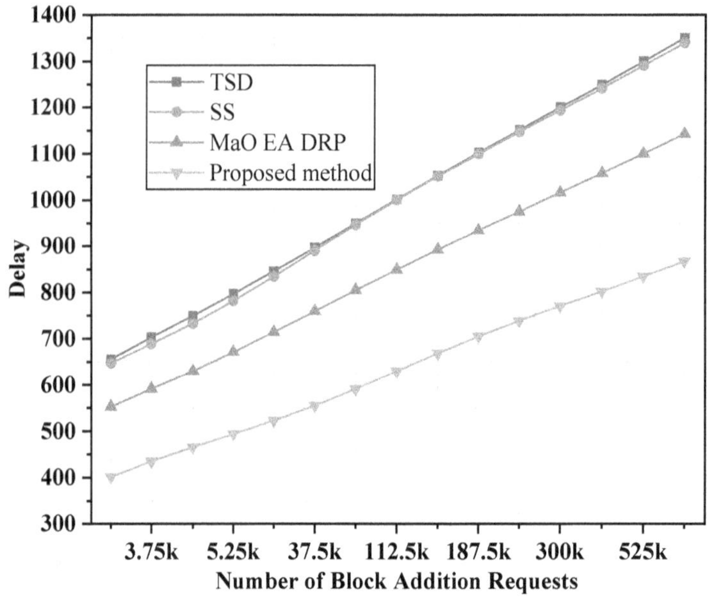

Fig. 5.5 Average delay during mining using sidechains.

proposed sidechaining, which facilitates the selection of low-energy communication nodes and is the root cause of the improvement. Using Mayfly Optimizer to divide large blockchains into smaller chains improves performance and facilitates the use of intelligent sharding techniques for real-time deployments.

The Mayfly Optimizer is one instrument that facilitates the introduction of sophisticated sharding algorithms. Fig.5.5 below displays the results of a similar calculation on the amount of time needed for communications during various communication types.

Fig.5.5. and the accompanying analysis show that the suggested model is superior to TSD (Yun et al. 2019), SS (Zheng, Xu, Luo, Zheng, Zheng, Chen, Zhou, Yan and Zhang 2022), and MaO EA DRP (Cai et al. 2021) in terms of communication energy delay reduction by 14.5%, 10.4%, and 18.5%, respectively. Each of these percentages represents a delay that was accomplished by TSD (Yun et al. 2019), SS (Zheng, Xu, Luo, Zheng, Zheng, Chen, Zhou, Yan and Zhang 2022), and MaO EA DRP (Cai et al. 2021).

This advantage is a direct outcome of joining the chains using distance measurements, which is done using low-complexity sidechains. When a single-chained blockchain's performance suffers, adopting the MO Model to divide it into several smaller chains is a viable set of solutions. This makes it easier to build smart sharding algorithms for real-time deployments, which improves performance in general. Additionally, Fig.5.6 displays the processes that were used to determine the MER for each transaction.

This research, together with Fig.5.6. demonstrates that under different situations, the suggested model may achieve a MER of communication that is 3.9% higher than TSD (Yun et al. 2019), 3.1% higher than SS (Zheng, Xu, Luo, Zheng, Zheng, Chen,

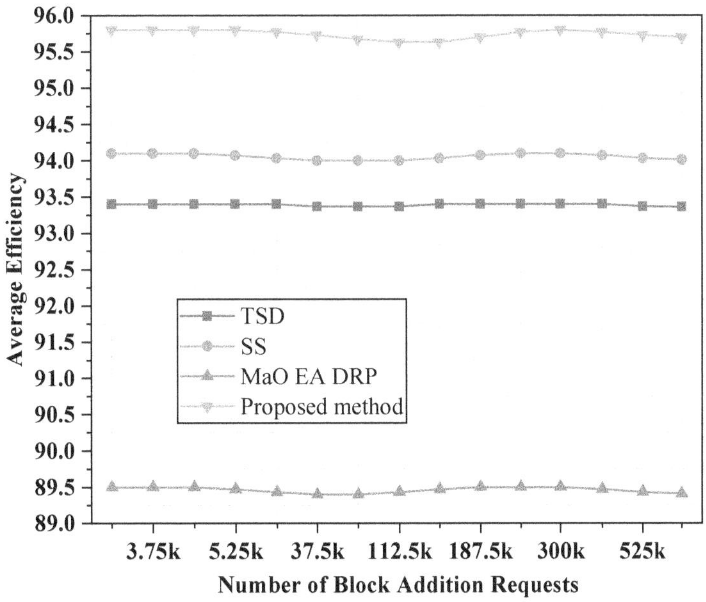

Fig. 5.6 Average Mining efficiency using sidechains.

Zhou, Yan and Zhang 2022), and 8.3% higher than MaO EA DRP (Cai et al. 2021).

The proposed optimization, which chooses sidechains according to temporal MER levels, is directly responsible for this improvement. If you want to implement sophisticated sharding algorithms for real-time deployments, which are aided by the partitioning of single-chained blockchains into smaller chains using Mayfly Optimizer, then you'll see a speed boost. In order to facilitate the implementation of smart sharding algorithms, Mayfly Optimizer is one of the resources that may be used. These improvements have increased the network's efficiency, and the supplied architecture may be put to use in setting up large-scale networks for real-time applications.

The proposed model uses the Mayfly Optimization (MO) Method to evaluate the temporal mining performance (of miners) in terms of throughput of mining, block mining ratio, delay, and energy needed for mining operations. These metrics are combined to generate a fitness function that aids in determining whether block-chains should merge or split. During split operations, blockchains are divided into two equal parts, while merge operations store blockchains for future retrieval. To validate the performance of the model, it was simulated under standard conditions using Network Simulator 2 (NS2.34). The throughput evaluation revealed that the proposed model outperforms TSD (Yun et al. 2019) by 8.5%, SS (Zheng, Xu, Luo, Zheng, Zheng, Chen, Zhou, Yan and Zhang 2022) by 6.0%, and MaO EA DRP (Cai et al. 2021) by 10.4% across a wide range of communication scenarios.

The acceptance of the MO Model, which divides enormous blockchains into smaller ones, could make the implementation of intelligent sharding methods for use in real-time possible. This adoption will result in the previously indicated improvement. In a variety of communication situations, additional evaluation reveals that the proposed model may achieve an overall energy consumption that is 6.4% lower than TSD (Yun et al. 2019), 4.5% lower than SS (Zheng, Xu, Luo, Zheng, Zheng, Chen, Zhou, Yan and Zhang 2022), and 12.2% lower than MaO EA DRP (Cai et al. 2021). The implementation of the proposed sidechaining, which facilitates the selection of low-energy communication nodes and is the cause of the advancement, makes this improvement feasible. Using Mayfly Optimizer to divide large blockchains into smaller chains enhances performance and enables the application of intelligent sharding techniques for real-time deployments. The Mayfly Optimizer is a tool that facilitates the development of sophisticated sharding algorithms. In terms of communication energy delay reduction, the proposed model is also superior to TSD (Yun et al. 2019), SS Zheng, Xu, Luo, Zheng, Zheng, Chen, Zhou, Yan and Zhang (2022), and MaO EA DRP (Cai et al. 2021) by 14.5%, 10.4%, and 18.0%, respectively. Each of these percentages represents a delay executed by TSD (Yun et al. 2019), SS (Zheng, Xu, Luo, Zheng, Zheng, Chen, Zhou, Yan and Zhang 2022), or MaO EA DRP (Cai et al. 2021).

This benefit is a direct result of joining the chains using distance measurements, which is accomplished using sidechains with low complexity. When the performance of a single-chained blockchain suffers, adopting the MO Model to divide it into multiple smaller chains is a viable solution. This facilitates the development of intelligent sharding algorithms for real-time deployments, thereby improving overall performance. The proposed model may achieve an MER of communication that is 3.9% higher than TSD (Yun et al. 2019), 3.1% higher than SS (Zheng, Xu, Luo, Zheng, Zheng, Chen, Zhou, Yan and Zhang 2022), and 8.3% higher than MaO EA DRP (Cai et al. 2021) under various communication conditions. This enhancement is directly attributable to the proposed optimization, which selects sidechains based on their temporal MER levels. If you want to implement sophisticated sharding algorithms for real-time deployments, which are aided by the partitioning of single-chained blockchains into smaller chains using Mayfly Optimizer, then you will experience a performance increase. Mayfly Optimizer is one of the available resources that can be used to facilitate the implementation of smart sharding algorithms. These enhancements have increased the network's efficacy, and the provided architecture can be used to create large-scale networks for real-time applications.

5.4 Summary

To sum up, the Mayfly Optimisation (MO) Model that has been suggested offers notable improvements in performance for blockchain-based Internet of Things healthcare implementations. The MO Method is used by the model to assess mining performance in terms of throughput, block mining ratio, delay, and energy consumption. The fitness function that establishes whether or not blockchains should split or merge is created using these metrics. Simulation results using Network Simulator 2 (NS2.34) under standard conditions show that the suggested model performs better in multiple communication scenarios than the current models, including TSD, SS, and MaO EA DRP. Compared to TSD, SS, and MaO EA DRP, it achieves 8.5%, 6.0%, and 10.4% higher throughput, respectively. Furthermore, compared to equivalent models, the model uses 6,4%, 4.5%, and 12.2% less energy. Additionally, compared to TSD, SS, and MaO EA DRP, it reduces communication energy delay by 14.5%, 10.4%, and 18.0%, respectively. Furthermore, the model attains greater mining efficiency rates (MER) for various scenarios compared to TSD, SS, and MaO EA DRP by 3.9%, 3.1%, and 8.3%, respectively.

The suggested model allows for the sidechaining of large blockchains to create smaller chains, which allows intelligent sharding algorithms to be deployed in real time. This improves overall performance, reduces communication delay, and uses less energy. According to the results, implementing the MO Model enhances network performance and qualifies it for widespread real-time healthcare applications. In summary, the suggested MO Model made possible by the Mayfly Optimizer offers a viable way to boost the security and effectiveness of blockchain-based IoT healthcare deployments, leading to better processes for communication delay reduction, energy efficiency, and performance. The performance of this model needs to be evaluated in larger scenarios in the future. It can be enhanced by integrating hybrid bioinspired techniques, such as Bacterial Foraging Optimisation (BFO), Grey Wolf Optimisation (GWO), and others, for various scenarios. Deep learning models can also be integrated by researchers to identify the best sidechains even in the face of widespread attacks.

CHAPTER 6

Conclusion

6.1 Recap of Key Findings

Throughout the course of this thesis, a comprehensive exploration of healthcare security using the integration of Internet of Things (IoT), blockchain, and machine learning (ML) has yielded a wealth of key findings. These findings represent significant contributions to the field of healthcare security and serve as a testament to the potential of emerging technologies in safeguarding patient data, enhancing care delivery, and mitigating security threats. The following section provides a recap of the key findings presented in this thesis:

1. **Multi-layered Security Models**: The research has showcased the effectiveness of multi-layered security models that combine blockchain-based data integrity with real-time threat detection powered by ML. These models provide a robust defense against a wide range of security threats in healthcare environments.

2. **Blockchain for Data Integrity**: Blockchain technology has emerged as a foundational element in ensuring data integrity, access control, and transparency in healthcare systems. Its immutable ledger design protects the security of electronic health records (EHRs) and IoT data, lowering the risk of manipulation and illegal access.

3. **Real-time Threat Detection**: The integration of ML algorithms has enabled real-time threat detection and response, offering healthcare providers the ability to identify security breaches and anomalies promptly. ML-driven analytics enhance patient safety and the integrity of healthcare data.

4. **Adaptive Security Measures**: Dynamic and adaptive security measures, informed by metaheuristic algorithms, have demonstrated the capability to respond to evolving threats and adapt to changing network conditions. These measures ensure security resilience and minimize vulnerabilities.

5. **IoT Empowerment**: IoT devices have empowered remote patient monitoring, personalized treatment plans, and data-driven decision-making. However, they

have also introduced new security challenges, which can be effectively addressed through the integration of blockchain and ML technologies.

6. **Lightweight Security Solutions**: Recognizing the resource constraints often present in healthcare settings, the research has emphasized the development of lightweight security solutions that optimize resource consumption without compromising security effectiveness.

7. **Global Healthcare Interoperability**: The research emphasizes the importance of global healthcare interoperability, facilitated by blockchain-based data exchange and standardized data formats. Interoperable healthcare systems enable international collaboration and research.

8. **Patient-Centric Security**: Patient trust and empowerment have been central themes in the research findings. Patient-centric security measures ensure that individuals can actively participate in their healthcare management while having confidence in data confidentiality and integrity.

In summary, the key findings presented in this thesis underscore the transformative potential of integrating IoT, blockchain, and ML in healthcare security. These findings provide a roadmap for enhancing security practices, preserving patient privacy, and enabling data-driven healthcare in an increasingly digitized world. As healthcare continues to evolve, the insights gained from this research will guide the development of secure, patient-centric, and adaptable healthcare systems.

6.2 Contributions to Healthcare Security

The research conducted in this thesis has made significant contributions to the field of healthcare security, advancing the understanding and practice of safeguarding patient data, ensuring data integrity, and mitigating security threats. These contributions encompass a broad spectrum of areas and represent a synthesis of innovative approaches and technologies. The following section highlights the key contributions made to healthcare security through this research:

1. **Integrated Security Framework**: This thesis presents an integrated security architecture that leverages the combined potential of IoT, blockchain, and machine learning (ML) technologies. The framework takes a comprehensive approach to healthcare security, covering data integrity, real-time threat detection, and adaptive security solutions.

2. **Blockchain for Data Integrity**: The research underscores the pivotal role of blockchain technology in preserving data integrity within healthcare systems. By

leveraging blockchain's immutable ledger architecture, healthcare organizations can ensure the tamper-resistance and transparency of electronic health records (EHRs) and IoT data.

3. **Real-time Threat Detection**: The integration of ML algorithms for real-time threat detection and anomaly identification represents a groundbreaking contribution. These algorithms empower healthcare providers to promptly identify security breaches and respond proactively, safeguarding patient safety and data integrity.

4. **Adaptive Security Measures**: The development of dynamic and adaptive security measures, guided by metaheuristic algorithms, provides a novel approach to healthcare security. These measures enable healthcare systems to adapt to evolving threats, ensuring security resilience and reducing vulnerabilities.

5. **IoT Empowerment**: This research showcases the transformative potential of IoT devices in healthcare, enabling remote patient monitoring, personalized treatment plans, and data-driven insights. Simultaneously, it addresses the associated security challenges, offering solutions to mitigate risks.

6. **Lightweight Security Solutions**: The emphasis on developing lightweight security solutions tailored to resource-constrained healthcare settings is a significant contribution. These solutions optimize resource consumption while maintaining robust security, making them practical and sustainable.

7. **Privacy-Preserving ML**: The research highlights the importance of preserving patient privacy while leveraging ML for data analytics. Privacy-preserving machine learning approaches, such as federated learning and homomorphic encryption, help to strike the difficult balance between data value and privacy protection.

8. **Usability and User Training**: Recognizing the critical role of healthcare professionals in security practices, this research provides recommendations for enhancing usability and establishing comprehensive training programs. These contributions bridge the gap between technology and healthcare practice.

9. **Global Healthcare Interoperability**: The emphasis on global healthcare interoperability, enabled by blockchain-based data exchange and standardized data formats, facilitates international collaboration and research. This contribution is particularly relevant in the context of global healthcare challenges.

10. **Patient-Centric Security**: The research underscores the significance of patient-centric security measures, fostering patient trust and empowerment. Patients are

motivated to engage actively in the administration of their healthcare, secure in the knowledge that their information will remain confidential and reliable.

In summary, this thesis's contributions to healthcare security are multifaceted and far-reaching. They provide a roadmap for healthcare organizations and researchers to enhance security practices, embrace emerging technologies, and ensure that patient data remains secure, private, and accessible. The holistic approach presented here represents a significant step toward a future where healthcare security is synonymous with adaptability, transparency, and patient-centricity.

6.3 Practical Implications and Future Scopes

The findings and insights derived from this thesis have substantial practical implications for healthcare providers, policymakers, researchers, and technology developers. Additionally, they point to promising avenues for future research and innovation. This section explores the practical implications of the research and outlines potential future scopes:

6.3.1 Practical Implications

- Enhanced Data Security: Healthcare organizations can implement the integrated security framework proposed in this research to enhance data security. By adopting blockchain for data integrity and ML for real-time threat detection, they can safeguard electronic health records (EHRs) and IoT data against tampering and unauthorized access.

- Patient-Centric Care: The patient-centric security measures highlighted in this research can foster patient trust and engagement. Healthcare providers can empower patients with secure access to their health data, promoting active participation in their healthcare decisions.

- Resource-Efficient Security: Resource-constrained healthcare settings can benefit from the development of lightweight security solutions. These solutions offer robust security without imposing excessive computational or energy burdens, ensuring sustainability.

- Global Collaboration: Healthcare systems and organizations can leverage blockchain-based data exchange and standardized data formats to enable global collaboration in research and patient care. This promotes international partnerships and data sharing for addressing global healthcare challenges.

- Privacy-Preserving Analytics: The adoption of privacy-preserving ML techniques allows healthcare providers to extract valuable insights from patient data while adhering to stringent privacy regulations. This enables data-driven decision-making without compromising individual privacy.

- Usability and Training: Usability enhancements and comprehensive training programs can bridge the gap between technology and healthcare practice. Healthcare professionals can effectively use and manage secure systems, ensuring smooth integration into their workflows.

6.3.2 Future Scopes

- Blockchain Interoperability: Further research can explore blockchain interoperability protocols to facilitate seamless data exchange among heterogeneous healthcare systems. Interoperable blockchains would enable cross-border data sharing and collaboration.

- Privacy-Preserving AI: Future research can delve deeper into the development of ethical and privacy-preserving AI models for healthcare applications. Ensuring that AI algorithms are free from bias and adhere to ethical principles is crucial.

- Scalable Blockchain Solutions: Research efforts can focus on enhancing blockchain scalability to accommodate the growing volume of healthcare data generated by IoT devices. Scalable blockchain solutions are essential for the continued growth of healthcare systems.

- Real-time Threat Intelligence: Advancements in real-time threat intelligence platforms can further enhance healthcare security. These platforms can continuously monitor network traffic and device behavior to detect and respond to emerging threats.

- Cross-Disciplinary Collaboration: Encouraging cross-disciplinary collaboration among healthcare professionals, data scientists, and cybersecurity experts can drive innovative solutions to complex healthcare security challenges.

- Ethical AI Governance: Establishing ethical AI governance frameworks in healthcare can ensure that AI models are trained and deployed with fairness, transparency, and accountability.

- Standardized Evaluation Metrics: Future research can work towards establishing industry-standard benchmarks and evaluation metrics for healthcare security solutions. Standardized metrics enable consistent performance assessments.

In conclusion, the practical implications of this research extend to the implementation of robust healthcare security measures, patient-centric care, and resource-efficient solutions. Simultaneously, the future scopes indicate exciting opportunities for further research and innovation in healthcare security. By embracing these implications and pursuing future scopes, stakeholders can contribute to a secure, patient-centric, and technologically advanced healthcare ecosystem.

6.4 Overall Summary and Final Remarks

In this comprehensive exploration of healthcare security, this thesis has navigated the intricate landscape of safeguarding patient data, enhancing care delivery, and mitigating security threats. By integrating Internet of Things (IoT), blockchain, and machine learning (ML) technologies, we have embarked on a transformative journey that holds immense promise for the future of healthcare security. In this final section, we provide an overall summary of the thesis and offer concluding remarks that encapsulate its significance.

Summary of the Thesis: Throughout the thesis, we embarked on a multidimensional journey that began with an analysis of remote health monitoring-based IoT security models. We delved into the nuances of data security, privacy preservation, and threat mitigation, recognizing the complexity that surrounds healthcare security in a digital age. As the thesis unfolded, we introduced innovative solutions and methodologies that address these complexities head-on.

Key findings emphasized the central role of blockchain technology in preserving data integrity, ML's real-time threat detection capabilities, and the importance of adaptive security measures. Lightweight security solutions tailored to resource-constrained healthcare settings were recommended, as were patient-centric security measures to empower individuals in their healthcare journey. Privacy-preserving ML techniques were explored, underscoring the delicate balance between data utility and privacy protection.

The research highlighted the need for usability enhancements and comprehensive training programs to bridge the gap between technology and healthcare practice. We emphasized the importance of global healthcare interoperability, facilitated by blockchain-based data exchange and standardized data formats, and underscored the significance of patient trust and empowerment in patient-centric security.

Final Remarks: As we conclude this journey, it is essential to reflect on the overarching significance of the research conducted. Our exploration of healthcare security using IoT, blockchain, and ML technologies has yielded a synthesis of innovative approaches and practical insights. We have not only addressed the immediate challenges facing healthcare security but have also contributed to shaping the future of secure, patient-centric, and adaptable healthcare systems.

In this era of rapid digital transformation, healthcare security is paramount. Patients entrust healthcare providers with their most sensitive and personal information, and the responsibility to safeguard this data is non-negotiable. The solutions proposed in this thesis provide a blueprint for achieving this goal. Blockchain technology stands as an immutable guardian of data integrity, while ML offers real-time vigilance against evolving threats. Together, they create a dynamic and adaptive security ecosystem that empowers healthcare providers to deliver the highest standard of care. Moreover, our emphasis on patient-centric security recognizes that individuals are not passive recipients of healthcare but active participants in their well-being. By providing patients with secure access to their health data, we empower them to make informed decisions and actively engage in their healthcare journey.

While we celebrate the achievements of this thesis, we acknowledge that the field of healthcare security is ever-evolving. New challenges will arise, and innovative technologies will emerge. As such, we offer this thesis as a stepping stone—a foundation upon which future researchers and healthcare professionals can build. The practical implications and future scopes outlined in this conclusion provide a roadmap for continued progress in healthcare security.

In closing, the fusion of IoT, blockchain, and ML technologies represents a beacon of hope in the quest for a secure and patient-centric healthcare ecosystem. With unwavering dedication to data integrity, privacy, and innovation, we can navigate the complexities of healthcare security with confidence and lead the way toward a healthier and safer future for all scenarios.

REFERENCES

Ahad, A., Tahir, M. and Yau, K.-L. A. (2019), '5g-based smart healthcare network: architecture, taxonomy, challenges and future research directions', *IEEE access* **7**, 100747–100762.

Ahmad, M., Jabbar, S., Ahmad, A., Piccialli, F. and Jeon, G. (2018), 'A sustainable solution to support data security in high bandwidth healthcare remote locations by using tcp cubic mechanism', *IEEE Transactions on Sustainable Computing* **5**(2), 249–259.

Ahmad, R. and Alsmadi, I. (2021), 'Machine learning approaches to iot security: A systematic literature review', *Internet of Things* **14**, 100365.

Al-Garadi, M. A., Mohamed, A., Al-Ali, A. K., Du, X., Ali, I. and Guizani, M. (2020), 'A survey of machine and deep learning methods for internet of things (iot) security', *IEEE Communications Surveys and Tutorials* **22**(3), 1646–1685.

Alam, M. S., Husain, D., Naqvi, S. and Kumar, P. (2018), Iot security through machine learning and homographic encryption technique, *in* 'International Conference on New Trends in Engineering and Technology (ICNTET), Chennai'.

Algarni, A. (2019), 'A survey and classification of security and privacy research in smart healthcare systems', *IEEE Access* **7**, 101879–101894.

Alladi, T., Chamola, V. et al. (2020), 'Harci: A two-way authentication protocol for three entity healthcare iot networks', *IEEE Journal on Selected Areas in Communications* **39**(2), 361–369.

Allifah, N. M. and Zualkernan, I. A. (2022), 'Ranking security of iot-based smart home consumer devices', *IEEE Access* **10**, 18352–18369.

Alsubaei, F., Abuhussein, A., Shandilya, V. and Shiva, S. (2019), 'Iomt-saf: Internet of medical things security assessment framework', *Internet of Things* **8**, 100123.

Amato, F., Casola, V., Cozzolino, G., De Benedictis, A. and Moscato, F. (2019), 'Exploiting workflow languages and semantics for validation of security policies in iot composite services', *IEEE Internet of Things Journal* **7**(5), 4655–4665.

Anjum, N., Alibakhshikenari, M., Rashid, J., Jabeen, F., Asif, A., Mohamed, E. M. and Falcone, F. (2022), 'Iot-based covid-19 diagnosing and monitoring systems: A survey', *Ieee Access* **10**, 87168–87181.

Anwar, M., Abdullah, A. H., Qureshi, K. N. and Majid, A. H. (2017), 'Wireless body area networks for healthcare applications: An overview', *TELKOMNIKA (Telecommunication Computing Electronics and Control)* **15**(3), 1088–1095.

Asheralieva, A. and Niyato, D. (2021), 'Throughput-efficient lagrange coded private blockchain for secured iot systems', *IEEE Internet of Things Journal* **8**(19), 14874–14895.

Aujla, G. S. and Jindal, A. (2020), 'A decoupled blockchain approach for edge-envisioned iot-based healthcare monitoring', *IEEE Journal on Selected Areas in Communications* **39**(2), 491–499.

Azeem, M., Ullah, A., Ashraf, H., Jhanjhi, N., Humayun, M., Aljahdali, S. and Tabbakh, T. A. (2021), 'Fog-oriented secure and lightweight data aggregation in iomt', *IEEE Access* **9**, 111072–111082.

Balthar, S., Kiran, R. and Sanath, S. (2018), 'Security for iot systems using machine learning', *Int. J. Adv. Res. Innov. Ideas Edu* **4**(2), 2707–2710.

Bao, Y., Qiu, W. and Cheng, X. (2021), 'Secure and lightweight fine-grained searchable data sharing for iot-oriented and cloud-assisted smart healthcare system', *IEEE Internet of Things Journal* **9**(4), 2513–2526.

Baracaldo, N., Chen, B., Ludwig, H., Safavi, A. and Zhang, R. (2018), Detecting poisoning attacks on machine learning in iot environments, *in* '2018 IEEE international congress on internet of things (ICIOT)', IEEE, pp. 57–64.

Bera, B., Das, A. K., Garg, S., Piran, M. J. and Hossain, M. S. (2021), 'Access control protocol for battlefield surveillance in drone-assisted iot environment', *IEEE Internet of Things Journal* .

Bera, B., Saha, S., Das, A. K. and Vasilakos, A. V. (2020), 'Designing blockchain-based access control protocol in iot-enabled smart-grid system', *IEEE Internet of Things Journal* **8**(7), 5744–5761.

Besher, K. M., Subah, Z. and Ali, M. Z. (2020), 'Iot sensor initiated healthcare data security', *IEEE Sensors Journal* **21**(10), 11977–11982.

Bharati, S. and Podder, P. (2022), 'Machine and deep learning for iot security and privacy: applications, challenges, and future directions', *Security and Communication Networks* **2022**, 1–41.

Bhattacharya, P., Tanwar, S., Bodkhe, U., Tyagi, S. and Kumar, N. (2019), 'Bindaas: Blockchain-based deep-learning as-a-service in healthcare 4.0 applications', *IEEE Transactions on Network Science and Engineering* **8**(2), 1242–1255.

Bhattacharya, P., Tanwar, S., Shah, R. and Ladha, A. (2020), Mobile edge computing-enabled blockchain framework—a survey, *in* 'Proceedings of ICRIC 2019', Springer, pp. 797–809.

Bhattacharya, P., Tiwari, A. K., Verma, A., Tanwar, S. and Sharma, R. (n.d.), 'Lightblocks: A trusted lightweight signcryption and consensus scheme for industrial iot ecosystems', *Available at SSRN 4025114* .

Bhuiyan, M. N., Rahman, M. M., Billah, M. M. and Saha, D. (2021), 'Internet of things (iot): A review of its enabling technologies in healthcare applications, standards protocols, security, and market opportunities', *IEEE Internet of Things Journal* **8**(13), 10474–10498.

Bi, H., Liu, J. and Kato, N. (2021), 'Deep learning-based privacy preservation and data analytics for iot enabled healthcare', *IEEE Transactions on Industrial Informatics* **18**(7), 4798–4807.

Bkassiny, M., Li, Y. and Jayaweera, S. K. (2012), 'A survey on machine-learning techniques in cognitive radios', *IEEE Communications Surveys and Tutorials* **15**(3), 1136–1159.

Bradley, A. P. (1997), 'The use of the area under the roc curve in the evaluation of machine learning algorithms', *Pattern recognition* **30**(7), 1145–1159.

Branch, J. W., Giannella, C., Szymanski, B., Wolff, R. and Kargupta, H. (2013), 'In-network outlier detection in wireless sensor networks', *Knowledge and information systems* **34**, 23–54.

Buczak, A. L. and Guven, E. (2015), 'A survey of data mining and machine learning methods for cyber security intrusion detection', *IEEE Communications surveys and tutorials* **18**(2), 1153–1176.

Cai, X., Geng, S., Zhang, J., Wu, D., Cui, Z., Zhang, W. and Chen, J. (2021), 'A sharding scheme-based many-objective optimization algorithm for enhancing security in blockchain-enabled industrial internet of things', *IEEE Transactions on Industrial Informatics* **17**(11), 7650–7658.

Cano, M.-D. and Cañavate-Sanchez, A. (2020), 'Preserving data privacy in the internet of medical things using dual signature ecdsa', *Security and Communication Networks* **2020**.

Challa, S., Das, A. K., Kumar, N., Wu, F. and Vasilakos, A. (2018), 'Design and analysis of authenticated key agreement scheme in cloud-assisted cyber-physical systems', *Future Generation Computer Systems* **108**.

Chen, E., Zhu, Y., Zhou, Z., Lee, S.-Y., Wong, W. E. and Chu, W. C.-C. (2021), 'Policychain: A decentralized authorization service with script-driven policy on blockchain for internet of things', *IEEE Internet of Things Journal* .

Chen, M.-Y. (2021), 'Establishing a cybersecurity home monitoring system for the elderly', *IEEE Transactions on Industrial Informatics* **18**(7), 4838–4845.

Chen, R., Wang, L., Peng, C. and Zhu, R. (2022), 'An effective sharding consensus algorithm for blockchain systems', *Electronics* **11**(16), 2597.

Chinaei, M. H., Gharakheili, H. H. and Sivaraman, V. (2021), 'Optimal witnessing of healthcare iot data using blockchain logging contract', *IEEE Internet of Things Journal* **8**(12), 10117–10130.

Christo, M. S., Jesi, V. E., Priyadarsini, U., Anbarasu, V., Venugopal, H. and Karuppiah, M. (2021), 'Ensuring improved security in medical data using ecc and blockchain technology with edge devices', *Security and Communication Networks* **2021**.

Das, A. K., Bera, B., Saha, S., Kumar, N., You, I. and Chao, H.-C. (2021), 'Ai-envisioned blockchain-enabled signature-based key management scheme for industrial cyber–physical systems', *IEEE Internet of Things Journal* **9**(9), 6374–6388.

Das, A. K., Wazid, M., Yannam, A. R., Rodrigues, J. J. and Park, Y. (2019), 'Provably secure ecc-based device access control and key agreement protocol for iot environment', *IEEE Access* **7**, 55382–55397.

Dean, J. and Ghemawat, S. (2008), 'Mapreduce: simplified data processing on large clusters', *Communications of the ACM* **51**(1), 107–113.

Deebak, B. D. and Al-Turjman, F. (2020), 'Smart mutual authentication protocol for cloud based medical healthcare systems using internet of medical things', *IEEE Journal on Selected Areas in Communications* **39**(2), 346–360.

Deebak, B. D., Al-Turjman, F., Aloqaily, M. and Alfandi, O. (2019), 'An authentic-based privacy preservation protocol for smart e-healthcare systems in iot', *IEEE Access* **7**, 135632–135649.

Diro, A. A. and Chilamkurti, N. (2018), 'Distributed attack detection scheme using deep learning approach for internet of things', *Future Generation Computer Systems* **82**, 761–768.

Dorri, A., Kanhere, S. S., Jurdak, R. and Gauravaram, P. (2017), Blockchain for iot security and privacy: The case study of a smart home, *in* '2017 IEEE international conference on pervasive computing and communications workshops (PerCom workshops)', IEEE, pp. 618–623.

Dorri, A., Kanhere, S. S., Jurdak, R. and Gauravaram, P. (2019), 'Lsb: A lightweight scalable blockchain for iot security and anonymity', *Journal of Parallel and Distributed Computing* **134**, 180–197.

Doshi, R., Apthorpe, N. and Feamster, N. (2018), Machine learning ddos detection for consumer internet of things devices, *in* '2018 IEEE Security and Privacy Workshops (SPW)', IEEE, pp. 29–35.

Egala, B. S., Pradhan, A. K., Badarla, V. and Mohanty, S. P. (2021), 'Fortified-chain: a blockchain-based framework for security and privacy-assured internet of medical things with effective access control', *IEEE Internet of Things Journal* **8**(14), 11717–11731.

Elayan, H., Aloqaily, M. and Guizani, M. (2021), 'Sustainability of healthcare data analysis iot-based systems using deep federated learning', *IEEE Internet of Things Journal* **9**(10), 7338–7346.

Elhachmi, J. and Kobbane, A. (2022), 'Blockchain-based security mechanisms for internet of medical things (iomt)', *International Journal of Computer Networks and Communications* pp. 115–136.

Elhoseny, M. and Shankar, K. (2019), 'Reliable data transmission model for mobile ad hoc network using signcryption technique', *IEEE Transactions on Reliability* **69**(3), 1077–1086.

Farris, I., Taleb, T., Khettab, Y. and Song, J. (2018), 'A survey on emerging sdn and nfv security mechanisms for iot systems', *IEEE Communications Surveys and Tutorials* **21**(1), 812–837.

Fernández-Caramés, T. M. (2019), 'From pre-quantum to post-quantum iot security: A survey on quantum-resistant cryptosystems for the internet of things', *IEEE Internet of Things Journal* **7**(7), 6457–6480.

Gao, Y., Lin, H., Chen, Y. and Liu, Y. (2021), 'Blockchain and sgx-enabled edge-computing-empowered secure iomt data analysis', *IEEE Internet of Things Journal* **8**(21), 15785–15795.

Garg, N., Petwal, R., Wazid, M., Singh, D., Das, A. K. and Rodrigues, J. J. (2022), 'On the design of an ai-driven secure communication scheme for internet of medical things environment', *Digital Communications and Networks* .

Garg, N., Wazid, M., Das, A. K., Singh, D. P., Rodrigues, J. J. and Park, Y. (2020), 'Bakmp-iomt: Design of blockchain enabled authenticated key management protocol for internet of medical things deployment', *IEEE Access* **8**, 95956–95977.

Ghorpade, S. N., Zennaro, M., Chaudhari, B. S., Saeed, R. A., Alhumyani, H. and Abdel-Khalek, S. (2021), 'A novel enhanced quantum pso for optimal network configuration in heterogeneous industrial iot', *IEEE Access* **9**, 134022–134036.

Ghubaish, A., Salman, T., Zolanvari, M., Unal, D., Al-Ali, A. and Jain, R. (2020), 'Recent advances in the internet-of-medical-things (iomt) systems security', *IEEE Internet of Things Journal* **8**(11), 8707–8718.

Gope, P., Gheraibia, Y., Kabir, S. and Sikdar, B. (2020), 'A secure iot-based modern healthcare system with fault-tolerant decision making process', *IEEE Journal of Biomedical and Health Informatics* **25**(3), 862–873.

Griggs, K. N., Ossipova, O., Kohlios, C. P., Baccarini, A. N., Howson, E. A. and Hayajneh, T. (2018), 'Healthcare blockchain system using smart contracts for secure automated remote patient monitoring', *Journal of medical systems* **42**(7), 1–7.

Gull, S., Parah, S. A. and Muhammad, K. (2020), 'Reversible data hiding exploiting huffman encoding with dual images for iomt based healthcare', *Computer Communications* **163**, 134–149.

Hady, A. A., Ghubaish, A., Salman, T., Unal, D. and Jain, R. (2020), 'Intrusion detection system for healthcare systems using medical and network data: A comparison study', *IEEE Access* **8**, 106576–106584.

Hafid, A., Hafid, A. S. and Samih, M. (2020), 'Scaling blockchains: A comprehensive survey', *IEEE Access* **8**, 125244–125262.

Hamza, R., Yan, Z., Muhammad, K., Bellavista, P. and Titouna, F. (2020), 'A privacy-preserving cryptosystem for iot e-healthcare', *Information Sciences* **527**, 493–510.

Han, D., Zhu, Y., Li, D., Liang, W., Souri, A. and Li, K.-C. (2021), 'A blockchain-based auditable access control system for private data in service-centric iot environments', *IEEE Transactions on Industrial Informatics* .

Han, G., Xiao, L. and Poor, H. V. (2017), Two-dimensional anti-jamming communication based on deep reinforcement learning, *in* '2017 IEEE international conference on acoustics, speech and signal processing (ICASSP)', IEEE, pp. 2087–2091.

Hasan, M. K., Islam, S., Sulaiman, R., Khan, S., Hashim, A.-H. A., Habib, S., Islam, M., Alyahya, S., Ahmed, M. M., Kamil, S. et al. (2021), 'Lightweight encryption technique to enhance medical image security on internet of medical things applications', *IEEE Access* **9**, 47731–47742.

Hasan, M. Z. and Al-Turjman, F. (2017), 'Optimizing multipath routing with guaranteed fault tolerance in internet of things', *IEEE Sensors Journal* **17**(19), 6463–6473.

Hassija, V., Chamola, V., Saxena, V., Jain, D., Goyal, P. and Sikdar, B. (2019), 'A survey on iot security: application areas, security threats, and solution architectures', *IEEE Access* **7**, 82721–82743.

He, H. and Garcia, E. A. (2009), 'Learning from imbalanced data', *IEEE Transactions on knowledge and data engineering* **21**(9), 1263–1284.

Hong, Z., Guo, S. and Li, P. (2022), 'Scaling blockchain via layered sharding', *IEEE Journal on Selected Areas in Communications* **40**(12), 3575–3588.

Huang, C., Wang, Z., Chen, H., Hu, Q., Zhang, Q., Wang, W. and Guan, X. (2020), 'Repchain: A reputation-based secure, fast, and high incentive blockchain system via sharding', *IEEE Internet of Things Journal* **8**(6), 4291–4304.

Huang, H., Yue, Z., Peng, X., He, L., Chen, W., Dai, H.-N., Zheng, Z. and Guo, S. (2022), 'Elastic resource allocation against imbalanced transaction assignments in sharding-based permissioned blockchains', *IEEE Transactions on Parallel and Distributed Systems* **33**(10), 2372–2385.

Hussain, F., Hussain, R., Hassan, S. A. and Hossain, E. (2020), 'Machine learning in iot security: Current solutions and future challenges', *IEEE Communications Surveys and Tutorials* **22**(3), 1686–1721.

Indumathi, J., Shankar, A., Ghalib, M. R., Gitanjali, J., Hua, Q., Wen, Z. and Qi, X. (2020), 'Block chain based internet of medical things for uninterrupted, ubiquitous, user-friendly, unflappable, unblemished, unlimited health care services (bc iomt u 6 hcs)', *IEEE Access* **8**, 216856–216872.

Iqbal, M. and Matulevičius, R. (2021), 'Exploring sybil and double-spending risks in blockchain systems', *IEEE Access* **9**, 76153–76177.

Iqbal, W., Abbas, H., Daneshmand, M., Rauf, B. and Bangash, Y. A. (2020), 'An in-depth analysis of iot security requirements, challenges, and their countermeasures via software-defined security', *IEEE Internet of Things Journal* **7**(10), 10250–10276.

Islam, N., Farhin, F., Sultana, I., Kaiser, M. S., Rahman, M. S., Mahmud, M., SanwarHosen, A. and Cho, G. H. (2021), 'Towards machine learning based intrusion detection in iot networks.', *Computers, Materials and Continua* **69**(2).

Ismail, W. N., Hassan, M. M., Alsalamah, H. A. and Fortino, G. (2020), 'Cnn-based health model for regular health factors analysis in internet-of-medical things environment', *IEEE Access* **8**, 52541–52549.

Iwaya, L. H., Ahmad, A. and Babar, M. A. (2020), 'Security and privacy for mhealth and uhealth systems: A systematic mapping study', *IEEE Access* **8**, 150081–150112.

Jagdish, M., Anand, N., Gaurav, K., Bashir, S., Alqahtani, A. and Saravanan, V. (2022), 'Multihoming big data network using blockchain-based query optimization scheme', *Wireless Communications and Mobile Computing* **2022**.

Ji, W., Xu, J., Qiao, H., Zhou, M. and Liang, B. (2019), 'Visual iot: Enabling internet of things visualization in smart cities', *IEEE Network* **33**(2), 102–110.

Jiang, Q., Zhang, N., Ni, J., Ma, J., Ma, X. and Choo, K.-K. R. (2020), 'Unified biometric privacy preserving three-factor authentication and key agreement for cloud-assisted autonomous vehicles', *IEEE Transactions on Vehicular Technology* **69**(9), 9390–9401.

Jin, H., Dai, X., Xiao, J., Li, B., Li, H. and Zhang, Y. (2021), 'Cross-cluster federated learning and blockchain for internet of medical things', *IEEE Internet of Things Journal* **8**(21), 15776–15784.

Jolfaei, A. A., Aghili, S. F. and Singelee, D. (2021), 'A survey on blockchain-based iomt systems: Towards scalability', *Ieee Access* **9**, 148948–148975.

Karie, N. M., Sahri, N. M., Yang, W., Valli, C. and Kebande, V. R. (2021), 'A review of security standards and frameworks for iot-based smart environments', *IEEE Access* .

Khan, A. Y., Latif, R., Latif, S., Tahir, S., Batool, G. and Saba, T. (2019), 'Malicious insider attack detection in iots using data analytics', *IEEE Access* **8**, 11743–11753.

Khan, S. F. (2017), Health care monitoring system in internet of things (iot) by using rfid, *in* '2017 6th International conference on industrial technology and management (ICITM)', IEEE, pp. 198–204.

Kim, S. (2019), 'Two-phase cooperative bargaining game approach for shard-based blockchain consensus scheme', *IEEE Access* **7**, 127772–127780.

Kulkarni, R. V. and Venayagamoorthy, G. K. (2009), Neural network based secure media access control protocol for wireless sensor networks, *in* '2009 international joint conference on neural networks', IEEE, pp. 1680–1687.

Kumar, A., Krishnamurthi, R., Nayyar, A., Sharma, K., Grover, V. and Hossain, E. (2020), 'A novel smart healthcare design, simulation, and implementation using healthcare 4.0 processes', *IEEE Access* **8**, 118433–118471.

Kumari, A., Gupta, R., Tanwar, S. and Kumar, N. (2020), 'Blockchain and ai amalgamation for energy cloud management: Challenges, solutions, and future directions', *Journal of Parallel and Distributed Computing* **143**, 148–166.

Lara, E., Aguilar, L., Sanchez, M. A. and García, J. A. (2020), 'Lightweight authentication protocol for m2m communications of resource-constrained devices in industrial internet of things', *Sensors* **20**(2).
URL: *https://www.mdpi.com/1424-8220/20/2/501*

Le, T.-V., Lu, C.-F., Hsu, C.-L., Do, T. K., Chou, Y.-F. and Wei, W.-C. (2022), 'A novel three-factor authentication protocol for multiple service providers in 6g-aided intelligent healthcare systems', *IEEE Access* **10**, 28975–28990.

Lee, S.-Y., Wi, S.-r., Seo, E., Jung, J.-K. and Chung, T.-M. (2017), Profiot: Abnormal behavior profiling (abp) of iot devices based on a machine learning approach, *in* '2017 27th International telecommunication networks and applications conference (ITNAC)', IEEE, pp. 1–6.

Lei, K., Du, M., Huang, J. and Jin, T. (2020), 'Groupchain: Towards a scalable public blockchain in fog computing of iot services computing', *IEEE Transactions on Services Computing* **13**(2), 252–262.

Li, J., Cai, J., Khan, F., Rehman, A. U., Balasubramaniam, V., Sun, J. and Venu, P. (2020), 'A secured framework for sdn-based edge computing in iot-enabled healthcare system', *IEEE Access* **8**, 135479–135490.

Li, X., Wang, Q., Lan, X., Chen, X., Zhang, N. and Chen, D. (2019), 'Enhancing cloud-based iot security through trustworthy cloud service: An integration of security and reputation approach', *IEEE Access* **7**, 9368–9383.

Liang, J., Qin, Z., Xue, L., Lin, X. and Shen, X. (2021), 'Efficient and privacy-preserving decision tree classification for health monitoring systems', *IEEE Internet of Things Journal* **8**(16), 12528–12539.

Liao, B., Ali, Y., Nazir, S., He, L. and Khan, H. U. (2020), 'Security analysis of iot devices by using mobile computing: a systematic literature review', *IEEE Access* **8**, 120331–120350.

Liu, H., Han, D. and Li, D. (2020), 'Fabric-iot: A blockchain-based access control system in iot', *IEEE Access* **8**, 18207–18218.

Liu, J., Li, X., Jiang, Q., Obaidat, M. S. and Vijayakumar, P. (2020), Bua: A blockchain-based unlinkable authentication in vanets, *in* 'ICC 2020-2020 IEEE International Conference on Communications (ICC)', IEEE, pp. 1–6.

Liu, L. and Li, Z. (2022), 'Permissioned blockchain and deep reinforcement learning enabled security and energy efficient healthcare internet of things', *IEEE Access* .

Liu, Y., Liu, L., Liang, J., Chai, J., Lei, X. and Zhang, H. (2020), 'High-performance long range-based medium access control layer protocol', *Electronics* **9**(8), 1273.

Liu, Y., Shan, G., Liu, Y., Alghamdi, A., Alam, I. and Biswas, S. (2022), 'Blockchain bridges critical national infrastructures: E-healthcare data migration perspective', *IEEE Access* **10**, 28509–28519.

Liu, Y., Yu, J., Fan, J., Vijayakumar, P. and Chang, V. (2021), 'Achieving privacy-preserving dsse for intelligent iot healthcare system', *IEEE Transactions on Industrial Informatics* **18**(3), 2010–2020.

Ma, Z., Wang, L. and Zhao, W. (2020), 'Blockchain-driven trusted data sharing with privacy protection in iot sensor network', *IEEE Sensors Journal* **21**(22), 25472–25479.

Malani, S., Srinivas, J., Das, A. K., Srinathan, K. and Jo, M. (2019), 'Certificate-based anonymous device access control scheme for iot environment', *IEEE Internet of Things Journal* **6**(6), 9762–9773.

Mandal, S., Bera, B., Sutrala, A. K., Das, A. K., Choo, K.-K. R. and Park, Y. (2020), 'Certificateless-signcryption-based three-factor user access control scheme for iot environment', *IEEE Internet of Things Journal* **7**(4), 3184–3197.

Masud, M., Gaba, G. S., Choudhary, K., Hossain, M. S., Alhamid, M. F. and Muhammad, G. (2021), 'Lightweight and anonymity-preserving user authentication scheme for iot-based healthcare', *IEEE Internet of Things Journal* **9**(4), 2649–2656.

Mehta, P., Gupta, R. and Tanwar, S. (2020), 'Blockchain envisioned uav networks: Challenges, solutions, and comparisons', *Computer Communications* **151**, 518–538.

Meidan, Y., Bohadana, M., Shabtai, A., Guarnizo, J. D., Ochoa, M., Tippenhauer, N. O. and Elovici, Y. (2017), Profiliot: A machine learning approach for iot device identification based on network traffic analysis, *in* 'Proceedings of the symposium on applied computing', pp. 506–509.

Meneghello, F., Calore, M., Zucchetto, D., Polese, M. and Zanella, A. (2019), 'Iot: Internet of threats? a survey of practical security vulnerabilities in real iot devices', *IEEE Internet of Things Journal* **6**(5), 8182–8201.

Meng, Y., Huang, Z., Shen, G. and Ke, C. (2019), 'Sdn-based security enforcement framework for data sharing systems of smart healthcare', *IEEE Transactions on Network and Service Management* **17**(1), 308–318.

Miettinen, M., Marchal, S., Hafeez, I., Asokan, N., Sadeghi, A.-R. and Tarkoma, S. (2017), Iot sentinel: Automated device-type identification for security enforcement in iot, *in* '2017 IEEE 37th international conference on distributed computing systems (ICDCS)', IEEE, pp. 2177–2184.

Mizrahi, A. and Rottenstreich, O. (2020), 'Blockchain state sharding with space-aware representations', *IEEE Transactions on Network and Service Management* **18**(2), 1571–1583.

Mohanta, B. K., Jena, D., Ramasubbareddy, S., Daneshmand, M. and Gandomi, A. H. (2020), 'Addressing security and privacy issues of iot using blockchain technology', *IEEE Internet of Things Journal* **8**(2), 881–888.

Mohanty, S. N., Ramya, K., Rani, S. S., Gupta, D., Shankar, K., Lakshmanaprabu, S. and Khanna, A. (2020), 'An efficient lightweight integrated blockchain (elib) model for iot security and privacy', *Future Generation Computer Systems* **102**, 1027–1037.

More, S., Singla, J., Verma, S., Ghosh, U., Rodrigues, J. J., Hosen, A. S., Ra, I.-H. et al. (2020), 'Security assured cnn-based model for reconstruction of medical images on the internet of healthcare things', *IEEE Access* **8**, 126333–126346.

Namvar, N., Saad, W., Bahadori, N. and Kelley, B. (2016), Jamming in the internet of things: A game-theoretic perspective, *in* '2016 IEEE Global Communications Conference (GLOBECOM)', IEEE, pp. 1–6.

Narudin, F. A., Feizollah, A., Anuar, N. B. and Gani, A. (2016), 'Evaluation of machine learning classifiers for mobile malware detection', *Soft Computing* **20**, 343–357.

Neshenko, N., Bou-Harb, E., Crichigno, J., Kaddoum, G. and Ghani, N. (2019), 'Demystifying iot security: An exhaustive survey on iot vulnerabilities and a first empirical look on internet-scale iot exploitations', *IEEE Communications Surveys and Tutorials* **21**(3), 2702–2733.

Nguyen, D. C., Pathirana, P. N., Ding, M. and Seneviratne, A. (2019), 'Blockchain for secure ehrs sharing of mobile cloud based e-health systems', *IEEE access* **7**, 66792–66806.

Nguyen, D. C., Pathirana, P. N., Ding, M. and Seneviratne, A. (2021), 'Bedgehealth: A decentralized architecture for edge-based iomt networks using blockchain', *IEEE Internet of Things Journal* **8**(14), 11743–11757.

Nguyen, L. D., Leyva-Mayorga, I., Lewis, A. N. and Popovski, P. (2021), 'Modeling and analysis of data trading on blockchain-based market in iot networks', *IEEE Internet of Things Journal* **8**(8), 6487–6497.

Nobakht, M., Sivaraman, V. and Boreli, R. (2016), A host-based intrusion detection and mitigation framework for smart home iot using openflow, *in* '2016 11th International conference on availability, reliability and security (ARES)', IEEE, pp. 147–156.

Oh, M.-K., Lee, S., Kang, Y. and Choi, D. (2019), 'Wireless transceiver aided run-time secret key extraction for iot device security', *IEEE Transactions on Consumer Electronics* **66**(1), 11–21.

Oktian, Y. E. and Lee, S.-G. (2020), 'Borderchain: blockchain-based access control framework for the internet of things endpoint', *IEEE Access* **9**, 3592–3615.

Patel, S. B., Bhattacharya, P., Tanwar, S. and Kumar, N. (2020), 'Kirti: A blockchain-based credit recommender system for financial institutions', *IEEE Transactions on Network Science and Engineering* **8**(2), 1044–1054.

Pyoung, C. K. and Baek, S. J. (2019), 'Blockchain of finite-lifetime blocks with applications to edge-based iot', *IEEE Internet of Things Journal* **7**(3), 2102–2116.

Qu, Y., Zheng, G., Ma, H., Wang, X., Ji, B. and Wu, H. (2019), 'A survey of routing protocols in wban for healthcare applications', *Sensors* **19**(7), 1638.

Rachakonda, L., Bapatla, A. K., Mohanty, S. P. and Kougianos, E. (2020), 'Sayopillow: Blockchain-integrated privacy-assured iomt framework for stress management considering sleeping habits', *IEEE Transactions on Consumer Electronics* **67**(1), 20–29.

Rahman, A., Islam, M. J., Rahman, Z., Reza, M. M., Anwar, A., Mahmud, M. P., Nasir, M. K. and Noor, R. M. (2020), 'Distb-condo: Distributed blockchain-based iot-sdn model for smart condominium', *IEEE Access* **8**, 209594–209609.

Ramzan, S., Aqdus, A., Ravi, V., Koundal, D., Amin, R. and Al Ghamdi, M. A. (2022), 'Healthcare applications using blockchain technology: Motivations and challenges', *IEEE Transactions on Engineering Management* .

Rathore, S., Park, J. H. and Chang, H. (2021), 'Deep learning and blockchain-empowered security framework for intelligent 5g-enabled iot', *IEEE Access* **9**, 90075–90083.

Ray, P. P., Chowhan, B., Kumar, N. and Almogren, A. (2021), 'Biothr: electronic health record servicing scheme in iot-blockchain ecosystem', *IEEE Internet of Things Journal* **8**(13), 10857–10872.

Ren, J., Li, J., Liu, H. and Qin, T. (2021), 'Task offloading strategy with emergency handling and blockchain security in sdn-empowered and fog-assisted healthcare iot', *Tsinghua Science and Technology* **27**(4), 760–776.

Ren, W., Sun, Y., Luo, H. and Guizani, M. (2021), 'Siledger: A blockchain and abe-based access control for applications in sdn-iot networks', *IEEE Transactions on Network and Service Management* **18**(4), 4406–4419.

Rezaeibagha, F., Mu, Y., Huang, K. and Chen, L. (2020), 'Secure and efficient data aggregation for iot monitoring systems', *IEEE Internet of Things Journal* **8**(10), 8056–8063.

Rinki, K., Verma, P. and Singh, R. K. (2022), 'A novel matrix multiplication based lsb substitution mechanism for data security and authentication', *Journal of King Saud University-Computer and Information Sciences* **34**(8), 5510–5524.

Rocha, L. M., Cappabianco, F. A. and Falcão, A. X. (2009), 'Data clustering as an optimum-path forest problem with applications in image analysis', *International Journal of Imaging Systems and Technology* **19**(2), 50–68.

Sabrina, F., Li, N. and Sohail, S. (2022), 'A blockchain based secure iot system using device identity management', *Sensors* **22**(19), 7535.

Saied, A., Overill, R. E. and Radzik, T. (2016), 'Detection of known and unknown ddos attacks using artificial neural networks', *Neurocomputing* **172**, 385–393.

Sairam, R., Bhunia, S. S., Thangavelu, V. and Gurusamy, M. (2019), 'Netra: Enhancing iot security using nfv-based edge traffic analysis', *IEEE Sensors Journal* **19**(12), 4660–4671.

Samaila, M. G., Sequeiros, J. B., Simoes, T., Freire, M. M. and Inacio, P. R. (2020), 'Iot-harpseca: A framework and roadmap for secure design and development of devices and applications in the iot space', *IEEE Access* **8**, 16462–16494.

Samuel, O., Omojo, A. B., Mohsin, S. M., Tiwari, P., Gupta, D. and Band, S. S. (2022), 'An anonymous iot-based e-health monitoring system using blockchain technology', *IEEE Systems Journal* .

Sathyadevan, S., Achuthan, K., Doss, R. and Pan, L. (2019), 'Protean authentication scheme–a time-bound dynamic keygen authentication technique for iot edge nodes in outdoor deployments', *IEEE access* **7**, 92419–92435.

Saxena, R. and Rao, D. S. (2023), Secured health monitoring system using optimized block chain framework, *in* '2023 International Conference on Circuit Power and Computing Technologies (ICCPCT)', IEEE, pp. 1097–1102.

Shabbir, M., Shabbir, A., Iwendi, C., Javed, A. R., Rizwan, M., Herencsar, N. and Lin, J. C.-W. (2021), 'Enhancing security of health information using modular encryption standard in mobile cloud computing', *IEEE Access* **9**, 8820–8834.

Shafiq, M., Tian, Z., Bashir, A. K., Du, X. and Guizani, M. (2020), 'Corrauc: a malicious bot-iot traffic detection method in iot network using machine-learning techniques', *IEEE Internet of Things Journal* **8**(5), 3242–3254.

Shi, C., Liu, J., Liu, H. and Chen, Y. (2017), Smart user authentication through actuation of daily activities leveraging wifi-enabled iot, *in* 'Proceedings of the 18th ACM international symposium on mobile ad hoc networking and computing', pp. 1–10.

Shin, D., Yun, K., Kim, J., Astillo, P. V., Kim, J.-N. and You, I. (2019), 'A security protocol for route optimization in dmm-based smart home iot networks', *IEEE Access* **7**, 142531–142550.

Siboni, S., Sachidananda, V., Meidan, Y., Bohadana, M., Mathov, Y., Bhairav, S., Shabtai, A. and Elovici, Y. (2019), 'Security testbed for internet-of-things devices', *IEEE transactions on reliability* **68**(1), 23–44.

Singh, S., Hosen, A. S. and Yoon, B. (2021), 'Blockchain security attacks, challenges, and solutions for the future distributed iot network', *IEEE Access* **9**, 13938–13959.

Sood, K., Karmakar, K. K., Yu, S., Varadharajan, V., Pokhrel, S. R. and Xiang, Y. (2019), 'Alleviating heterogeneity in sdn-iot networks to maintain qos and enhance security', *IEEE Internet of Things Journal* **7**(7), 5964–5975.

Srinivas, J., Das, A. K., Kumar, N. and Rodrigues, J. J. (2018), 'Cloud centric authentication for wearable healthcare monitoring system', *IEEE Transactions on Dependable and Secure Computing* **17**(5), 942–956.

Srinivas, J., Das, A. K., Wazid, M. and Vasilakos, A. V. (2020), 'Designing secure user authentication protocol for big data collection in iot-based intelligent transportation system', *IEEE Internet of Things Journal* **8**(9), 7727–7744.

Srivastava, R., BHATTACHARYA, P. and TIWARI, A. K. (2019), 'Dual buffers optical based packet switch incorporating arrayed waveguide gratings', *Journal of Engineering Research* **7**(1).

Su, Q., Zhang, R., Xue, R. and Li, P. (2020), 'Revocable attribute-based signature for blockchain-based healthcare system', *IEEE Access* **8**, 127884–127896.

Suarez, J., Quevedo, J., Vidal, I., Corujo, D., Garcia-Reinoso, J. and Aguiar, R. L. (2016), 'A secure iot management architecture based on information-centric networking', *Journal of Network and Computer Applications* **63**, 190–204.

Sun, S., Du, R., Chen, S. and Li, W. (2021), 'Blockchain-based iot access control system: towards security, lightweight, and cross-domain', *IEEE Access* **9**, 36868–36878.

Sun, Y., Lo, F. P.-W. and Lo, B. (2019), 'Security and privacy for the internet of medical things enabled healthcare systems: A survey', *IEEE Access* **7**, 183339–183355.

Tahsien, S. M., Karimipour, H. and Spachos, P. (2020), 'Machine learning based solutions for security of internet of things (iot): A survey', *Journal of Network and Computer Applications* **161**, 102630.

Tanwar, S., Bhatia, Q., Patel, P., Kumari, A., Singh, P. K. and Hong, W.-C. (2019), 'Machine learning adoption in blockchain-based smart applications: The challenges, and a way forward', *IEEE Access* **8**, 474–488.

Tian, Z., Li, M., Qiu, M., Sun, Y. and Su, S. (2019), 'Block-def: A secure digital evidence framework using blockchain', *Information Sciences* **491**, 151–165.

Vangala, A., Sutrala, A. K., Das, A. K. and Jo, M. (2021), 'Smart contract-based blockchain-envisioned authentication scheme for smart farming', *IEEE Internet of Things Journal* **8**(13), 10792–10806.

Wang, D., Bai, B., Lei, K., Zhao, W., Yang, Y. and Han, Z. (2019), 'Enhancing information security via physical layer approaches in heterogeneous iot with multiple access mobile edge computing in smart city', *IEEE Access* **7**, 54508–54521.

Wang, J., Hao, S., Wen, R., Zhang, B., Zhang, L., Hu, H. and Lu, R. (2020), 'Iot-praetor: Undesired behaviors detection for iot devices', *IEEE Internet of Things Journal* **8**(2), 927–940.

Wang, K., Chen, C.-M., Tie, Z., Shojafar, M., Kumar, S. and Kumari, S. (2021), 'Forward privacy preservation in iot-enabled healthcare systems', *IEEE transactions on industrial informatics* **18**(3), 1991–1999.

Wang, L., Ali, Y., Nazir, S. and Niazi, M. (2020), 'Isa evaluation framework for security of internet of health things system using ahp-topsis methods', *IEEE Access* **8**, 152316–152332.

Wang, N., Jiang, T., Lv, S. and Xiao, L. (2017), 'Physical-layer authentication based on extreme learning machine', *IEEE Communications Letters* **21**(7), 1557–1560.

Wang, X. and Jin, Z. (2019), 'An overview of mobile cloud computing for pervasive healthcare', *IEEE Access* **7**, 66774–66791.

Wang, Y., Su, Z., Ni, J., Zhang, N. and Shen, X. (2021), 'Blockchain-empowered space-air-ground integrated networks: Opportunities, challenges, and solutions', *IEEE Communications Surveys and Tutorials* .

Whaiduzzaman, M., Mahi, M. J. N., Barros, A., Khalil, M. I., Fidge, C. and Buyya, R. (2021), 'Bfim: Performance measurement of a blockchain based hierarchical tree layered fog-iot microservice architecture', *IEEE Access* **9**, 106655–106674.

Wold, S., Esbensen, K. and Geladi, P. (1987), 'Principal component analysis', *Chemometrics and intelligent laboratory systems* **2**(1-3), 37–52.

Wu, G., Wang, S., Ning, Z. et al. (2021), 'Blockchain-enabled privacy-preserving access control for data publishing and sharing in the internet of medical things', *IEEE Internet of Things Journal* **9**(11), 8091–8104.

Xi, J., Zou, S., Xu, G., Guo, Y., Lu, Y., Xu, J. and Zhang, X. (2021), 'A comprehensive survey on sharding in blockchains', *Mobile Information Systems* **2021**.

Xiao, L., Li, Y., Han, G., Liu, G. and Zhuang, W. (2016), 'Phy-layer spoofing detection with reinforcement learning in wireless networks', *IEEE Transactions on Vehicular Technology* **65**(12), 10037–10047.

Xiao, L., Li, Y., Huang, X. and Du, X. (2017), 'Cloud-based malware detection game for mobile devices with offloading', *IEEE Transactions on Mobile Computing* **16**(10), 2742–2750.

Xiao, L., Wan, X. and Han, Z. (2017), 'Phy-layer authentication with multiple landmarks with reduced overhead', *IEEE Transactions on Wireless Communications* **17**(3), 1676–1687.

Xiong, H., Jin, C., Alazab, M., Yeh, K.-H., Wang, H., Gadekallu, T. R., Wang, W. and Su, C. (2021), 'On the design of blockchain-based ecdsa with fault-tolerant batch verification protocol for blockchain-enabled iomt', *IEEE journal of biomedical and health informatics* **26**(5), 1977–1986.

Xu, G., Dong, J., Ma, C., Liu, J. and Cliff, U. G. O. (2022), 'A certificateless signcryption mechanism based on blockchain for edge computing', *IEEE Internet of Things Journal* .

Xu, J., Xue, K., Li, S., Tian, H., Hong, J., Hong, P. and Yu, N. (2019), 'Healthchain: A blockchain-based privacy preserving scheme for large-scale health data', *IEEE Internet of Things Journal* **6**(5), 8770–8781.

Xu, L., Zhou, X., Tao, Y., Liu, L., Yu, X. and Kumar, N. (2021), 'Intelligent security performance prediction for iot-enabled healthcare networks using an improved cnn', *IEEE Transactions on Industrial Informatics* **18**(3), 2063–2074.

Xu, X., Wang, X., Li, Z., Yu, H., Sun, G., Maharjan, S. and Zhang, Y. (2021), 'Mitigating conflicting transactions in hyperledger fabric-permissioned blockchain for delay-sensitive iot applications', *IEEE Internet of Things Journal* **8**(13), 10596–10607.

Yang, Q. and Wang, H. (2021), 'Privacy-preserving transactive energy management for iot-aided smart homes via blockchain', *IEEE Internet of Things Journal* **8**(14), 11463–11475.

Yang, X., Yang, X., Yi, X., Khalil, I., Zhou, X., He, D., Huang, X. and Nepal, S. (2021), 'Blockchain-based secure and lightweight authentication for internet of things', *IEEE Internet of Things Journal* .

Yin, X., Wang, S., Zhu, Y. and Hu, J. (2022), 'A novel length-flexible lightweight cancelable fingerprint template for privacy-preserving authentication systems in resource-constrained iot applications', *IEEE Internet of Things Journal* **10**(1), 877–892.

Yu, J., Lee, H., Kim, M.-S. and Park, D. (2008), 'Traffic flooding attack detection with snmp mib using svm', *Computer Communications* **31**(17), 4212–4219.

Yun, J., Goh, Y. and Chung, J.-M. (2019), 'Trust-based shard distribution scheme for fault-tolerant shard blockchain networks', *IEEE Access* **7**, 135164–135175.

Zaabar, B., Cheikhrouhou, O., Ammi, M., Awad, A. I. and Abid, M. (2021), Secure and privacy-aware blockchain-based remote patient monitoring system for internet of healthcare things, *in* '2021 17th International Conference on Wireless and Mobile Computing, Networking and Communications (WiMob)', IEEE, pp. 200–205.

Zaman, S., Khandaker, M. R., Khan, R. T., Tariq, F. and Wong, K.-K. (2022), 'Thinking out of the blocks: Holochain for distributed security in iot healthcare', *IEEE Access* **10**, 37064–37081.

Zeadally, S., Das, A. K. and Sklavos, N. (2021), 'Cryptographic technologies and protocol standards for internet of things', *Internet of Things* **14**, 100075.

Zhang, J., Wang, Y., Li, S. and Shi, S. (2020), 'An architecture for iot-enabled smart transportation security system: a geospatial approach', *IEEE Internet of Things Journal* **8**(8), 6205–6213.

Zhang, P., Wang, Y., Kumar, N., Jiang, C. and Shi, G. (2021), 'A security and privacy-preserving approach based on data disturbance for collaborative edge computing in social iot systems', *IEEE Transactions on Computational Social Systems* .

Zhang, Y., Li, B., Liu, B., Hu, Y. and Zheng, H. (2021), 'A privacy-aware pufs-based multiserver authentication protocol in cloud-edge iot systems using blockchain', *IEEE Internet of Things Journal* **8**(18), 13958–13974.

Zhang, Y., Liu, X., Luo, M. and Yang, C. (2019), 'Bio-inspired approach for long-range underwater navigation using model predictive control', *IEEE transactions on cybernetics* **51**(8), 4286–4297.

Zhang, Y., Sun, Y., Jin, R., Lin, K. and Liu, W. (2021), 'High-performance isolation computing technology for smart iot healthcare in cloud environments', *IEEE Internet of Things Journal* **8**(23), 16872–16879.

Zhao, J., Zhang, D., Liu, W., Qiu, X. and Brusic, V. (2022), 'Dht-based blockchain dual-sharding storage extension mechanism', *Applied Sciences* **12**(19), 9635.

Zhaofeng, M., Lingyun, W., Xiaochang, W., Zhen, W. and Weizhe, Z. (2019), 'Blockchain-enabled decentralized trust management and secure usage control of iot big data', *IEEE Internet of Things Journal* **7**(5), 4000–4015.

Zheng, P., Xu, Q., Luo, X., Zheng, Z., Zheng, W., Chen, X., Zhou, Z., Yan, Y. and Zhang, H. (2022), 'Aeolus: Distributed execution of permissioned blockchain transactions via state sharding', *IEEE Transactions on Industrial Informatics* .

Zheng, P., Xu, Q., Zheng, Z., Zhou, Z., Yan, Y. and Zhang, H. (2022), 'Meepo: Multiple execution environments per organization in sharded consortium blockchain', *IEEE Journal on Selected Areas in Communications* **40**(12), 3562–3574.

Zhu, F., Yi, X., Abuadbba, A., Khalil, I., Nepal, S. and Huang, X. (2021), 'Cost-effective authenticated data redaction with privacy protection in iot', *IEEE Internet of Things Journal* **8**(14), 11678–11689.

Zulkifl, Z., Khan, F., Tahir, S., Afzal, M., Iqbal, W., Rehman, A., Saeed, S. and Al-muhaideb, A. M. (2022), 'Fbashi: Fuzzy and blockchain-based adaptive security for healthcare iots', *IEEE Access* **10**, 15644–15656.

www.ingramcontent.com/pod-product-compliance
Lightning Source LLC
LaVergne TN
LVHW082344200926
848481LV00012B/3439
9798230326533